Joining God, Remaking Church, Changing the World

The New Shape of the Church in Our Time

ALAN J. ROXBURGH

Morehouse Publishing
NEW YORK

Morehouse Publishing, 19 East 34th Street, New York, NY 10016

Morehouse Publishing is an imprint of Church Publishing Incorporated.
www.churchpublishing.org

Cover art © 2014 Brian Whelan; www.brianwhelan.co.uk
Cover design by Laurie Klein Westhafer
Typeset by Rose Design

Library of Congress Cataloging-in-Publication Data

Roxburgh, Alan J.
 Joining God, remaking church, changing the world : the new shape of the church in our time / Alan J. Roxburgh.
    pages cm
 Includes bibliographical references.
 ISBN 978-0-8192-3211-3 (pbk.) -- ISBN 978-0-8192-3212-0 (ebook) 1. Mission of the church. 2. Church renewal. I. Title.
 BV601.8.R6885 2015
 253--dc23
                                          2015009370

Printed in the United States of America

Contents

Introduction

This book is written out of a community of men and women who've been on a journey together for more than a decade.[1] Together, we are seeking to understand and practice gospel life in our time. We are church leaders, teachers, consultants, parents, mothers, and fathers who connected in a common search for ways of being God's people in this time. We believe God's abundant Spirit is bringing new life to the church in North America, but it looks a lot different than we imagined when we started. We sense the Spirit calling us into a new imagination about being God's people.

Collectively, we've been involved in North American churches for more than one hundred years. Over that time we've participated in and witnessed fundamental changes in the ways church exists in our cultures. So many of the assumptions about church, such as it having a central place in people's lives, no longer hold. The questions churches are asking—like "How do we attract people?"—are not connecting with the actual people in our neighborhoods. It's clear to us that things are not going to go back to the way they were, either in the church or in our daily lives.

One natural and popular response is trying to fix the problems and make the church work through strategic plans, new techniques, and better programs. These approaches take up more and more energy but produce fewer and fewer results. This book is an invitation to join a different journey: to join what God is doing ahead of us in our neighborhoods and communities.

In these pages I hope to describe what we mean by "joining God in the neighborhood" and why it is so important. The Spirit is busy re-founding the church for our time, and every one of us is being

---

1. The group is formally known as The Missional Network. Learn more about us at *www.the missionalnetwork.com*. Many of the resources, stories, and strategies throughout this book come from our experience working with congregations and denominational bodies around the world.

invited to participate and discover what God is up to ahead of us. This begins with a commitment to place and discerning the presence of God in the everyday contexts where we work and live. These are the holy grounds where God is at work remaking our society and reweaving the fabric of our communities. Our role as followers of Jesus is joining the work God is already doing in the world.

There is great hope for the church in this movement, but it's a different imagination. We are confronted by a historic break from what church has meant for the past five hundred years. It's not so different from the break that occurred with the demise of the Roman Empire or in the European Protestant reformations. Such breaks call for the cultivation of a fundamentally different imagination, and this has huge implications for the rhythms of life and worship for Christian communities. Congregations are being invited to enter this open space and to confront the need for a changed imagination. This book describes what I've observed is required.

Change in God's Time

God worked through Abraham, Sarah, Isaac, Rebecca, Jacob, and Leah to shape a people who would become Israel. Their story took a dramatic turn when they were sent into slavery. It took another turn when, upon their release from captivity, they lost a generation while wandering in the wilderness. When their story seemed most hopeless, it turned one more time: "A long time passed, and the Egyptian king died. The Israelites were still groaning because of their hard work. They cried out, and their cry to be rescued from hard work rose up to God. God heard their cry of grief, and God remembered . . ." (Exodus 2:23–24).[2] The words announced a change in the world, and the message came to those with no reason to hope. God broke into their groaning and weeping, with news of a change.

In *City of God*, St. Augustine wrote: "God is always trying to give good things to us, but our hands are always too full to receive them." Like those Israelites, our hands can be too full with our fears and sense of loss for us to see or receive the good things God is doing

2. *Common English Bible* (Nashville: Christian Resources Development Corporation, 2010).

among us. Can we trust and open for these good things, even in the midst of our fear?

I would argue that, far from fearful times, we live in extraordinary times. I returned recently from a retreat weekend with our church, which meets at a house near our own in Vancouver. It is composed of people who live in the neighborhood as a way of being God's people. There are other such neighborhood-based Christian communities around the city, and we join together to listen, pray for our communities, and worship God. I'm continually surprised by the people who join. We're of all ages, from young children to people in their sixties. Many have come from congregations where we had to drive *to* church and where we were deeply invested in church programs and committees that obsessed with keeping the church itself going.

Why have we gathered? Not to get away from church—much of what we're learning has helped us to reimagine what church can be. We simply had this sense that God was stirring life in our neighborhoods, that the Spirit was moving within *and* beyond our conventional churches. We wanted to figure out how to join with God there. We love this journey of discovering what the Spirit is up to in our neighbor.

There are extraordinary, similar stories all around about how the Spirit is ahead of us, moving in the everydayness of our neighborhoods, if we just have the ears to hear them. These stories are taking place right next door and across the street, and I have the privilege of hearing and seeing them as I travel across North America, Europe, and the United Kingdom. It's not that any one of them on its own is world-transforming—that's not the point. But if you sit and listen to what's happening under the hype about church growth or the lament about denominational decline, you can hear the music of the Spirit, sounding a chord many of us dreamed of but never imagined would happen.

In one circle, I heard the story of a couple who had spent years being busy in their church to the extent that they had, literally, lost touch with the neighbors on their street. In a simple act of prayer and Scripture reading, they decided it was time to cross the lawn and knock on the door of the people who'd been living beside them for years. They baked cookies, arranged them on a plate, and made the odyssey across the lawn. They were greeted with total surprise—the neighbors had to wonder, "What do these people really want?" But they also heard gratitude. "Thank you so much! It's a bad time for us just now. J (the husband) has been diagnosed with cancer, and we're in the midst of chemotherapy." There was welcomed prayer at the door and, in God's amazing ways, the transformation of a neighborhood had begun.

One aging congregation found itself surrounded by new housing developments and shopping centers. Rather than wait for those new residents to discover them, they opted to partner with neighbors to plan community events like the town Winter Festival. Now these elder members are making new friends, discovering fresh energy, and launching plans for ministry *with* their neighbors, instead of *for* them. They're becoming a different kind of church.

Another friend told the story of how his wife wanted a table that could serve as a warm space for meals and conversation. He is not exactly "handy," but he had an acquaintance in the neighborhood skilled at carpentry. That friend volunteered to build the table. These relative strangers dwelt for a while around wood, saws, glue, and screws, until they wrought a wonderful table. But that is only half the story. Out of these conversations, an imagination was birthed: what if the table were a gift of the Spirit, a place around which the neighborhood could come to eat and talk and connect? The Spirit was plotting something good.

Such stories are the proof. The Spirit is moving like an underground stream, stirring relationship and inviting us to discover ways of being God's people that hardly fit the ways we've imagined being church in the recent past. The Spirit is disrupting and calling our churches into a new imagination about what it means to follow the way of Jesus.

And so, this is a book about hope. In the midst of massive social, cultural, economic, and structural upheavals at every level of life, many church leaders are struggling to make their churches work. At the very same time, God's Spirit is inviting a new imagination that is disruptive and energizing. Throughout Scripture and in the stories of God's people across history, these are exactly the kind of times when God's future breaks in with unimagined possibility. We are living in such a time.

From Church Questions to God Questions

We need to lay down and turn away from questions about how to fix the church or make it effective again and embrace a different kind of question: How do we discern what God is doing ahead of us in our neighborhoods and communities and join with God there?

Undergirding this question is the spirit of Lesslie Newbigin, an English missionary who spent decades leading global mission, only to return home and discover equally urgent challenges for the church in the West. Newbigin's writings from the 1960s to the 1980s formed the basis of the "missional movement" in North America: an effort to make God's mission the starting place for Christian community and life.

So far, the promise of that movement to transform churches on this continent has largely failed. This is because there is a malformed imagination at the center of North American church life. Newbigin framed the challenge in these terms: What would be involved in a missionary encounter between the gospel and this whole way of perceiving, thinking, and living we call "modern Western culture"?[3] For Newbigin, this question only made sense if God is the primary agent at work in the cultures of Europe and North America. This conviction has been lost in the major effort to engage a missional conversation in our time, mostly because we turned Newbigin's question back into what I think of as "church questions" (for example: How do we make the church more effective at reaching people? How can our church turn from inside to outside? What are the marks of a missional church?).

This default move laid bare a deformity in our imagination: we consistently make the church the subject and object of practically all our attention and energy. I am convinced that God's Spirit is using the disruptive unraveling facing so many congregations and denominations in order to call these churches to fundamentally change their focus and attention. This book is about that journey.

In order to go on this journey, we need to spend a bit of time mapping what's been happening to congregations and denominations over the past half-century. On that basis we can then discern the kind of journey onto which God is inviting us.

---

3. Lesslie Newbigin, *Foolishness to the Greeks* (Grand Rapids, MI: Eerdmans, 1986), 1.

On Seeing What Was Right in Front of Me

Jesus observed that the religious leaders of his day needed new eyes with which to see what was going on and new ears to hear what was happening. We have also become practiced at seeing what we want to see and hearing what we want to hear. Jesus was announcing the coming of a new reality that only some would be able to see and hear. In the midst of our great unraveling, the Spirit is calling the church toward a new way of being. The call is for us to have the eyes and ears to see and hear what God is doing in front of us. Can we see it?

Last summer I read David Eggers's *The Circle*,[4] a novel about how we learn to see, or not see, the world right in front of us. Eggers describes the shape of a potential networked world, a world of 24-hours-a-day/7-days-a-week technologies that lock us into a deformed, Orwellian-like society. Nearly everyone engages in group-think and group-speak. While the main character Mae descends further and further into this realm (the Circle), some see its malevolent implications and raise questions about the effects of a completely enmeshed, networked world. *The Circle*, as a morality play, is about what we choose to see and what we fail to see. It invites us to see our worlds through different eyes, to recover ways of seeing lost in a world overrun by screens and tweets.

That reality came home to me in a comical but strange way recently. My wife has lovingly told me over many years that, as an introvert, I spend too much time inside my own head and not enough seeing what is around me. When we were married some forty-five years ago, Jane was a public school teacher at the beginning of her career. At the end of her first year, a father, the senior executive of an international company, gave her three limited-edition Inuit prints in gratitude for her work with his son. We and our children eventually fell in love with the prints, and they became a central part of our home through several moves.

Two years ago we moved to a neighborhood where we could walk to everything, including church. Recently, Jane and I were sitting in the living room enjoying a relaxing evening. Suddenly, it struck me that for the past two years, I hadn't seen the prints. I asked: "Jane, where are the prints?" "Which prints?" she responded. "The

---

4. David Eggers, *The Circle* (New York: Vintage Books, 2013).

Inuit prints we've always had with us. You know the ones. I haven't seen them since we moved! What happened to them?" Jane thought I must be joking, but I insisted that I had no idea. Jane leaned forward and gently put her hand on my arm. "Alan, they're right here," she said, pointing at the long wall in front of us. "They're where we hung them when we moved in. How could you not see them?"

How could I not see what was right in front of me? In my intense busyness I simply missed things, even the ones that were precious and close by. We all fail to see, like Mae in Eggers's novel or the couple who did not notice that their next-door neighbors were struggling with cancer. The examples are endless. We become so engrossed in our own perceptions of what's important that we miss the wonder and presence of God in the lives around us.

Certain images, stories, or metaphors become so central to our life together that they shape everything, and we see little else. Eula Biss's recent book *On Immunity* illustrates this phenomenon perfectly.[5] At one level she explores the fears and reactions to immunizations of children, but at a deeper level she examines how we have allowed the image, or metaphor, of "inoculation" to characterize our whole lives. From helicopter parents to medical establishments, from strangers to everyday foods, we've become a society preoccupied with immunizing ourselves from any and all risks or the chance-filled vagaries of life. This tendency closes down imagination and creates, instead, a fear-based society.

I would not deny or dismiss the unprecedented challenges facing us—the social, climate, and economic transformation rocking our communities and congregations. But in the face of all this, I would propose an imagination very different from that of an "inoculation" story. I hope we can see abundance and possibility, even in the midst of upheaval. It is our choice how we read reality.

A Return to Hope

In part I of this book, I tell the story of the struggle that has marked reality for North American, mostly Protestant, churches and denominations descended from the European Reformations—what I call "the

---

5. Eula Biss, *On Immunity: An Inoculation* (Minneapolis: Grey Wolf Press, 2014).

unraveling." This accounting is not intended to be negative, but an invitation for us to see our vocation with renewed vision. Psalm 126 speaks these words of hope to a people who felt similarly defeated:

> When God restored the fortunes of Zion, we were like those who
>   dreamed.
> Our mouths were filled with laughter, our tongues with songs of joy.
> Then it was said among the nations, "The Lord has done great things
>   for them."
> The Lord has done great things for us and we are filled with joy.[6]

Can we see ourselves in a place where we can say, "God is doing great things and we are amazed?" This book is a pamphlet about that road to hope. I will try to avoid the technical or theological language of clergy and church leaders, though it will be impossible at times, since these make up my primary audience. The book begins with a description of what's been happening to us as congregations and denominations. It then argues that God isn't finished with these old denominations but is calling them onto a journey with Jesus for the sake of the world.

When Tolkien published *The Lord of the Rings* in 1954, he described it as "an act of rescue." He wanted to rescue a weary, discouraged people in the West from the hard, dark night that had fallen over them after the wars of the last century, so he told a beautiful story that began and ended in joy.[7] The characters traveled tough ground, and their illusions about the world were rudely dispelled, but they did return to that original ground: joy.

I have no pretense here to be Tolkien, but I desire to write a story that invites us to see again the joy and hope at the core of the Christian story. Like Tolkien's story, this will challenge our perceptions of what it means to be God's people. The Hobbits were forever transformed. There was no going back to the world they had known, but joy and fresh hope were waiting at the other side of the struggle.

Tolkien's story offers us another gift: he understood that God's future is not birthed in great leaders but in the small, sometimes

---

6. NIV, 2011.

7. J. R. R. Tolkien, "On Faery Stories," in *The Monster and the Critics and Other Essays* (Boston: Houghton Mifflin, 1984), 156.

hairy-toed, imperfectly shaped, ordinary people who may have no clue what is going on and no desire to go anywhere but within their own tight little worlds. These were the creatures who changed the world and, in the language of C. S. Lewis, were surprised by joy.

That is the journey onto which we are being invited, we who are engaged in the ordinary, imperfect churches God wants to use to create a new future. It requires a willingness from us to fundamentally reimagine what it means to be followers of Jesus, to be the church, to be the flawed ones through whom God will change the world. It is about looking for the truth of God's action in places very different from where we've been looking for the last century or more.

Imagining in the Real World

I firmly believe that an ordinary, local church can engage the big ideas of unraveling, of shifting from church-centered to God-centered questions, of joining the way of Jesus in their neighborhoods. The question is: How does this energizing call of the Spirit get practical and come alive on the ground? Part II of the book deals in depth with this question. As someone said a long time ago, most of us in congregations don't live in the world of big ideas and lofty dreams. We put our pants on one leg at a time, and we learn by watching how other people do things. And so I have sought to outline some basic, simple, concrete steps that can be taken by a congregation and clergy who put their pants on one leg at a time.

At the core of part II is the invitation to learn a new rhythm of congregational life. The practices outlined are not a new program that, if closely followed, will give churches the power to control their future. They introduce a way of forming each other in the way of Jesus, a way for introducing a new imagination into congregations. Changed imagination doesn't happen through a teaching series or reading a book on some hot new theme. It happens as a group of very ordinary men, women, and young people begin to take on new practices, in particular the practices of listening, discerning, experimenting, reflecting, and deciding. Together, these steps make up a journey. Obviously, there is much more to it than these five sets of practices, but they're the best place I know to begin.

Awake, Awake!

The Old Testament is full of stories of hope based in God's faithful action in the world. In 2 Kings 6:8–17, the king of Aram's troops were ranged against Israel seeking to capture Elisha, the prophet, in Dothan. The soldiers of Aram came at night and surrounded Dothan. Near dawn Elisha's aide went to the city walls, and upon seeing the army of Aram surrounding the city, he ran to Elisha in fear and despair. The servant could only see the facts and realities—the troops, the numbers, the bad news. He saw nothing else!

To this panic, Elisha responded, "Don't be afraid, because there are more of us than there are of them." Then he prayed, "Lord, please open the eyes that he may see." The Lord opened the servant's eyes, and he saw that the mountains were full of horses and fiery chariots surrounding Elisha.[8] Elisha's response was shaped by his capacity to see what his servant had missed. While his servant confessed trust in God, he did not act like it. Like the rest of Israel, he had no sense that God could or would be the active agent in the midst of this crisis.

As I will assert in the following chapters, a similar malformation has taken shape among many Christians in North America over the past half-century. We have come to see our sources of hope everywhere *except* in the reality of God's presence and action in our world. We might have claimed to be God's people, but we have accepted what might be called "modernity's wager"—on some level, we think life can be lived without God, that if we or our churches are to be saved, it is up to us alone.[9] This might sound like a strange claim if you regularly attend worship, but it is about the most basic convictions that have driven our actions.

Over the past half-century or more years, those congregations and denominations from the European migrations to the Americas have lived ever more deeply into a culture of radical individualism. We've become practiced at personalizing and psychologizing biblical stories for the purpose of self-help and generalized moral teaching

---

8. *Common English Bible.*

9. See Alan Seligman, *Modernity's Wager: Authority, the Self and Transcendence* (Princeton, NJ: Princeton University Press, 2003); and Susan E. Schreiner, *Are You Alone Wise?: The Search for Certainty in the Early Modern Era* (Oxford: Oxford University Press, 2011).

for being good citizens. We lost sight of the story that runs through Scripture about God's actions in the world.

What we actually need is to imagine that God is up to something. Imagine that God is active in the midst of what seems to be an unremitting unraveling of not just our churches but our way of life in North America. Imagine that the prophet Isaiah is speaking truth:

> Awake, awake
> put on your strength, Zion!
> Put on your splendid clothing,
> Jerusalem, you holy city;
> for the uncircumcised and unclean
> will no longer come into you.
> Shake the dust off yourself;
> rise up; sit enthroned, Jerusalem.
> Loose the bonds from your neck,
> captive Daughter of Zion!
>
> The Lord proclaims:
> You were sold for nothing,
> and you will be redeemed without money.
> The Lord God proclaims:
> Long ago my people went down
> to reside in Egypt.
> Moreover, Assyria has oppressed them without cause.
> And now what have I here? says the Lord.
> My people are taken away for nothing.
> Their rulers wail, says the Lord,
> and continually all day long my name is despised.
> Therefore, my people will know my name on that day;
> I am the one who promises it; I'm here.
>
> How beautiful upon the mountains
> are the feet of a messenger
> who proclaims peace,
> who brings good news,
> who proclaims salvation,
> who says to Zion, "Your God rules!" . . .

> Break into song together, you ruins of Jerusalem!
> The Lord has comforted his people and has redeemed
>   Jerusalem.
> The Lord has bared his holy arm in view of all the nations;
> all the ends of the earth have seen our God's victory.
>
> (Isaiah 52:1–7, 8–10)[10]

It's easy to lose sight of what's core to who we are, but Isaiah urges Israel to turn around. His prophecy isn't rooted in some generalized moral theory about human thriving or keeping the Golden Rule. It is grounded in the particular, concrete conviction that God is here. We are invited to embrace a fundamentally different reality where God is remaking the world and we are called to participate in that remaking.

For Isaiah there is no getting out of their predicament with the usual, established, calculated ways of doing things. There will be no expert, program, tactic, or strategy. The way forward requires a new way of seeing. This seeing calls the captives to remember their story. ("You were sold for nothing." "Long ago you went down to reside in Egypt." "My people will know my name.") That memory provides the clues to the truth: it is God who hears their cries and acts to change the situation.

Similarly, as Euro-tribal churches we need a radical reorientation of our eyes and our imagination. Listen, awaken, and hear the good news: "Your God reigns!" Ours is a time of hope. The Spirit is inviting us to turn from fear, from being depressed like those who have no hope and can't see anything beyond statistics and failed tactics. There's so much more going on. God is ahead, on the move, in the neighborhood.

---

10. *Common English Bible.*

PART I

The conversation is typical. You quickly sense the anxiety. On a phone or video conference, a team from a congregation or denominational office describes the challenge: how to make the change that will enable them to survive or grow again.

A denominational leader comes into town and wants a lunch meeting. As we catch up over sushi, he describes the situation in his region. Eventually he wonders if he needs to change to some other church, if they know something his group doesn't.

The staff of another denomination describes a growing percentage of congregations hovering on the edge of viability. They can't afford full-time clergy, and the people and their leaders are frozen with anxiety. Something has gone wrong, and people want answers.

I met with regional executives in Denver to discuss progress in a series of imaginative initiatives with some congregations. Little had happened. Not because they didn't want to see the initiatives go forward, but because their time and energy were consumed addressing an increasing number of conflicts and dysfunctions among churches and leaders.

While such stories are not true for every congregation or church leader, they are more and more the norm. What they demonstrate is that Protestant churches have been in the midst of a great unraveling for quite some time.

In order to step into hope realistically, we have to pause to understand how we got to this stage and just what the unraveling means. Isaiah reminds Israel how it got into the situation in which it found itself. Time and again, they gave over their lives and identities to Egypt. They lost covenant faithfulness, and ended up in the long Babylonian captivity. These events did not just happen to Israel. The people and their leaders participated. In each situation, they placed their hope in the tactics of power or survival.

But Isaiah does not recall these stories to badger Israel. He does so as part of proposing an alternative reality, one in which God is present and active in the midst of the unraveling. We, too, need to revisit the stories of what got us to this place of unraveling, in order to see the future God is shaping. Part I of this book outlines the contours of what has happened over the last half-century, while part II proposes ways we can be transformed.

This is the story of a great unraveling. I tell it to clear the ground so we can inhabit a different future.

CHAPTER ONE

The Great Unraveling

My wife loves to knit. I'm bemused as I watch her work. She will knit for hours and then, with a great sigh, unravel a week's worth of knitting. It's hard to watch.

In our story, what is coming undone is the long, cherished tradition of the "Euro-tribal churches" across North America. I use this term with great intention, and I'll take a moment to explain. The churches with which I have worked most closely and the ones with which this book deals most directly are those that trace to the great migrations from the United Kingdom and Europe over the past four to five hundred years, the churches that form the primary Christian groups in the United States and Canada. They created denominations shaped largely by ethnic and religious identities coming out of the fifteenth- and sixteenth-century reformations: Lutherans (Germany and Scandinavia), Episcopalians (England), Presbyterians (Scotland), United Church of Canada (Great Britain), Methodists and Baptists (England), Mennonites (the Netherlands and Germany), and so forth.

To a great extent these denominations were formed and expanded in the context of strong national and ethnic identities. For this reason, I characterize them as tribal and use the phrase Euro-tribal churches. It is important to note, but isn't the subject of this book, that these Euro-tribal churches morphed and created a good number of "made in the Americas" denominations, such as Churches of Christ, Pentecostalism, and indigenous spin-offs like National Baptists or the African Methodist Episcopal Church. These are highly nuanced developments, running alongside the Euro-tribal story. Likewise, it is clear that the Roman Catholic Church, in its own migrations to North America, had to redefine itself as one denomination among many others. For multiple reasons—perhaps because its liturgical tradition and hierarchy better transcend national-cultural identities—it has seemed able to weather the unraveling more cohesively than the Protestant denominations.

For the Euro-tribal churches, the story of this unraveling goes back to the middle of the last century. Sociologist Hugh McLeod explains the lead-up to the breakdown this way:

> In the 1940s and 1950s it was still possible to think of western Europe and North America as a "Christendom," in the sense that there were close links between religious and secular elites, that most children were socialized into membership in a Christian society, and that the church had a large presence in fields such as education and welfare, and a major influence on law and morality.[1]

The 1940s and 1950s, while influenced by fears of external threats from Communism, were a golden period for these churches. World War II had been won, the Great Depression was over, democracy was prevailing in the midst of a Cold War. The West was ready to celebrate, to leave behind the hardships of the previous half-century. Most Protestant churches flourished in this environment, where it seemed just about everyone and everything was Christian. These churches symbolized the public and social conscience of the age. They were the government, education, economic, and professional leaders of the nation at worship. Young families embraced the new suburbs, churches filled, and denominations experienced their greatest era of new church development.

In this milieu these churches can hardly be blamed for seeing themselves as the center of society and assuming their proclamations and actions would lead to the redemption and betterment of society. They pursued growth with gusto, expanding new church development, filling seminaries, and extending corporate denominational structures offering cradle-to-grave, branded programs that branched across the continent. Donald Luidens paints this picture:

> The corporate denomination "metaphor" . . . seems to be an apt representation of the organizational formula that saw

---

1. Hugh McLeod, *The Religious Crisis of the 1960s* (Oxford: Oxford University Press, 2007), 31.

the establishment and routinization of religious communions throughout the United States. The wide-open "religious marketplace" in the post-World War II era accelerated the development of this corporate model. Like competing businesses occupying a growing market niche, Protestant denominations around the country routinely perfected their production processes and marketing techniques. In these early years the level of competition was minimal and "success" was widespread. However, over time the religious marketplace became a crowded one, competition grew and success became elusive, which accelerated the transformation of the corporate denomination. . . .

[R]eflecting the imperialistic optimism of the age, the corporate model ushered in a worldwide vision for Christian ministry (symbolized in the title of the flagship Protestant journal of this era, the *Christian Century*). . . . The corporate model fuelled, and was in turn fuelled by, a Christianity that was outward-looking and expansionist.[2]

Few were aware of, or prepared for, the earthquakes to come. Just as the young church, after Pentecost, focused on reestablishing God's reign within the narrative of Jerusalem and Judaism and could not see the ways the Spirit was about to unravel most of its assumptions, so the denominations failed to see the massive dislocations into which the Spirit would soon deliver them.

The Protestant story couldn't hold the imagination or desires of post-war generations, so the '60s exploded like a socio-cultural-religious Mt. St. Helens. As McLeod observes: "In the religious history of the West these years may come to be seen as marking a rupture as profound as that brought about by the Reformation. . . . The 1960s was an international phenomenon."[3]

Throughout North America and Europe, we witnessed the Baby Boom, rising economic possibilities for huge swaths of the public, the Civil Rights Movement, the Vietnam War, the Sexual Revolution, the emergence of the self as the central source

2. See Donald A. Luidens in *Church, Identity and Change: Theology and Denominational Structures in Unsettled Times*, David A. Roozen and James R. Nieman, editors (Grand Rapids, MI: Eerdmans, 2005), 411–12.

3. Hugh McLeod, *The Religious Crisis of the 1960s* (Oxford: Oxford University Press, 2008), 1–3.

of meaning. Along with these came the Human Potential Movement, the Women's Movement, a shrinking world with expanded religious options, the end of National Service in the United Kingdom, the expansion of higher education from elites to the middle classes, the suburbanization of society, and the proliferation of new media.

The changes went on and on, and their impact was massive and unexpected. Like the Babylonian captivity or the destruction of Jerusalem in 70 CE, these events resulted in massive dislocation. The churches were thrown into a world for which they were unprepared. The natural instinct is to fix what is broken and to get back to the stability and predictability they had known. But that world had been torn up.

By the late 1960s numerical growth for the mainline denominations had come to a screeching halt. Despite warnings from observers of culture such as Peter Berger and Gibson Winter, the churches were largely unprepared. They continued expanding national staff, building national headquarters, and marketing their branded programs.

Protestant churches have only continued to lose their place in the emerging cultural milieu. If anything, the change has picked up pace, unabated, over the proceeding decades. Despite claims that conservative, evangelical churches had found the secret to growth, there is now sufficient evidence that the primary reason conservative churches grew was defections from mainline churches. The conservative Protestant churches have experienced their own unraveling tsunami, just a little later.

This unraveling has manifested most keenly as a progressive loss of connection between the churches and the generations that emerged from the 1960s onward. Here are some illustrations:

- If you were born between 1925 and 1945, there is a 60 percent chance you are in church today.
- If you were born between 1946 and 1964, there is a 40 percent chance you are in church today.
- If you were born between 1965 and 1983, there is a 20 percent chance you are in church today.
- If you were born after 1984, there is less than a 10 percent chance you are in church today.

1990–2005 Growth or Decline as a Percentage of the Population by Denominational Family

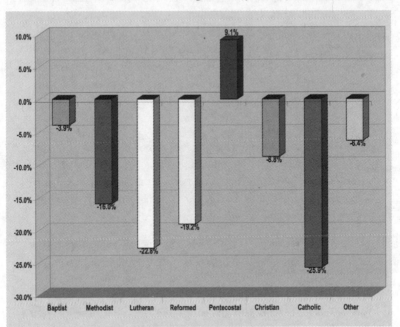

Good News in Unlikely Places

Ultimately, it is my strong contention that the Spirit has been at work in this long unraveling. The Spirit is inviting these churches to embrace a new imagination, but the other one had to unravel for us to see it for what it was. In this sense the malaise of our churches has been the work of God. Allow me to spell out several implications for this proposal:

> FIRST: If the Spirit has been at work in this long unraveling, then God is not done with the Euro-tribal, Protestant churches. In Scripture places of unraveling were preludes to God shaping a new future for God's people. For instance, the persecutions of Acts 8 precipitated a profoundly different church from the one the disciples imagined after Pentecost.

> SECOND: We are not in a contemporary or temporary "exile." Such language made sense to a generation that came to leadership

in the 1970s, but for the generations that followed, this is not some strange exilic land. Exile language is tinged with the eventuality that there's a way back. In truth, there is no returning, no going back. We are in a new location, a land many people call home, and so the churches must ask very different questions. Exile questions about how to fix and make the church work again won't help us to discern the Spirit.

THIRD: This space of unraveling is a space of hope. We are witnessing the Spirit preparing us for a new chapter in the story of God's mission. Our churches are at the end of a way of being God's people and at the beginning of something significantly different. It involves our awakening to an invitation that is not about fixing the church but a journey of exploration.

FOURTH: In this journey we are experiencing dislocation. More than adjustment, major change is required. The Spirit's invitation requires risk-taking, as we try on practices that will seem strange and awkward at first. It will ask us to change our basic sense of where God is at work. It will change our ideas about the location of God's actions.

FIFTH: We are embarking on a shared journey to discern what the Spirit is up to ahead of us in our neighborhoods and to join God in these places. How do we discern together? How do we join with God? How will this joining require us to be changed as a gathered people?

SIXTH: Like all new journeys we will need new ways of traveling. For Christians these ways are called *practices*. The final chapters of this book will explore several of them.

For these six reasons and lots more, I think the unraveling is God's good news for us. This is not the first time the Spirit has substantially disrupted the established patterns of the church's practice and place in a culture, and it will not be the last. Old Testament and New Testament examples abound. In addition, think of the disruption that happened when Christianity was formally designated the official religion of the Roman Empire—that dislocation led to the initiation of a rich desert monastic tradition. By the fifth and sixth centuries, Europe was in a period of massive social dislocation, and it sparked the emergence of new movements like the Celtic missionaries of the British Isles.

When I propose to groups that the great unraveling we're experiencing should be treated as an opportunity, and even as the work of the Spirit, the responses take several shapes. First, people reluctantly agree with the assessment. Then they take positions of resistance and critique. Many suggest the shifts in imagination and practice proposed in this book are too dramatic to be done in their churches or denominations. This response is understandable, and I don't dismiss it. What is required is a radical shift in the orientation of Christian life in North America.

I've come to this conviction after many years of wrestling with the question of Christian identity in societies rapidly removing the Christian narrative from the center of their lives. I work with denominational leaders of every stripe who tell me their members don't know how the Christian story forms a coherent narrative about what God is up to in the world or how we form our lives around it. As one bishop shared recently, his gut wrenches after visiting congregations and clergy. They know how to be kind and caring, but they don't know the Christian story. Congregants glue fragments of the story together with other bits from the media or latest trends in spirituality and self-help to blend their own, ever-shifting amalgam of beliefs and practices. There is a cry for discipleship programs or workshops to fix it all, but the problem lies at a much deeper level. The unraveling will not be resolved from within current assumptions about being God's people.

While I am not proposing the end of our churches or our traditions, congregational life and the role of clergy has to dramatically change. Congregations will still be the vital center where God's mission is worked out in our cities, towns, and villages. They are not going away. The unraveling is about a remaking of the church. This remaking is already underway.

The Unraveling Image

Because I have seen the resistance to the image of "unraveling," I want to spend a moment explaining why I think it's so crucial to understanding this stage in churches' lives.

Unraveling is a natural part of life.

Ways of life unravel over time. My wife travels to Ontario from Vancouver several times a year, and the trips increase as her parents age into their late nineties. With each visit Jane sees her mom and dad losing capacities they once took for granted. They once loved traveling, but it's too difficult for them to fly no matter how easy we try to make it. Painful as it is to watch, we know it is natural and appropriate. They are aging, they are changing, and our life with them is unraveling.

When my granddaughter Maddie was born in 2007, someone crocheted a baby blanket for her. Maddie and the blanket became inseparable. Over the years "Blanky" has gone through the washer and dryer more times than anyone can remember. Thanks to all those cycles, Blanky is irrevocably coming apart. My wife and daughter have tried to sew the fraying edges back together, but they won't win this one. Recently, ominous holes have appeared in the middle. Blanky is unraveling.

None of us celebrate this. Blanky has been a vital part of Maddie's growing up, especially when her mom was battling cancer. There is security, history, comfort, warmth, and just plain normalcy about having Blanky around, and we would like to fix the holes. But Maddie will soon have to adapt to life without Blanky by her side.

The new wine needs new wineskins.

It is not that the ways we have been God's people were wrong. They were developed for another time, and now they are fraying, stretched and torn in the midst of massive social change. This was, in part, why Jesus spoke of wineskins and new wine (Matthew 9:16–17). He did not say we need to throw away our traditions. If we know anything about wine, we know the new wine isn't always great. Good wine needs to sit for years before it matures and is ready to be enjoyed. But sometimes wineskins lose their capacity to stretch.

What I have to say is far from a simplistic celebration of the new. It's not a call to embrace the latest and greatest fads in worship or clergy training. But our imaginations as Christians got stuck in particular ways of being God's people. We have poured our energy into trying to repair the old wineskins, while the Spirit was pointing us in a different direction.

Unraveling must inspire more than grief.

Ours is not just any unraveling: it is a great unraveling, for something precious and enormously important to us has come apart and can no longer be woven back together. Those church traditions emanating from the European reformations have nurtured and shaped our imaginations for more than four centuries, and that imagination has in turn shaped a whole way of life, given us our identities, and provided us with ways of reading and navigating worlds. This precious heritage has had a long run near the center of Western societies. We are effectively at the end of that long period.

Given this truth, commentators regularly observe that we're experiencing loss and need significant time and space to walk through the stages of grief before we can move forward. I used to agree but not any longer. Some grieving will go on for a little longer, but this cannot be the primary response. Grief belongs to those who have lived long and deeply into the Euro-tribal churches' stories, and to those who have yoked themselves to that identity. But if the church's glory days were at least forty years ago, that means the generations without these memories are the majority. The only story they know is the unraveling, although they have heard much of life before the unraveling and may grieve alongside older leaders. Still, these new generations come with different experiences and expectations, and we need their leadership to challenge the primacy of the narrative of grief and fixing.

There's no use trying to explain the unraveling.

Loss produces the need for explanation. Some talk about the end of Christendom. Others speak of a "post"-something age (such as, post-Christian or post-denominational). But this is not particularly helpful. As theologian Graham Ward once said, placing the modifier "post" in front of an abstract noun doesn't render that noun any clearer but symbolizes a loss of explanations for what has occurred to us.[4] Still others say secularization is the culprit, but I find that theory

---

4. Graham Ward, *The Politics of Discipleship* (Grand Rapids, MI: Baker Academic, 2009), 154–55.

questionable. We simply don't live in a world of unbelief. Ours is a time when the opposite is true: people are yearning to believe in something, but the churches have little power to capture their attention.

If such explanations aren't sufficient, what do we do? What if we ask how these churches have actually addressed this unraveling over the past half-century? Attending to what we have been doing in the midst of this unraveling will tell us about the convictions out of which we operate. If we can name some of these convictions, we can propose alternative pathways for addressing the crisis. This is our task in the next chapter.

CHAPTER TWO

Reactions to the Unraveling (or "What Have We Done?")

[T]he key to dealing with a real crisis, one that goes beyond our personal realities, is in our abilities to move outside what we think of as normal. If the crisis is big enough, we have to reconsider the narrative or we can be destroyed by it.

—John Ralston Saul, *The Comeback*[1]

Actions are never neutral. They're freighted with unexamined assumptions about how things get done. This means actions tell more about our beliefs, convictions, and motivations than written confessions and stated beliefs. We will misidentify the appropriate pathway to the extent that we can't tell these truths about what we have done and why we've done it.[2]

For this reason, this chapter offers a summary of what the Euro-tribal churches have done to address the unraveling from the '60s to the present. It is suggestive rather than comprehensive, a high-level map showing the major contours of the terrain we have traveled.

This period parallels my own entry into the church world and my ordination as a pastor. In the early '70s while I was in graduate school studying to teach philosophy, God called me to the church. On completing a Master of Divinity degree, I took my first post in a small town. Looking back, I see that I entered as the unraveling began to really take hold. From then until the present, these Protestant Euro-tribal churches have been the arena of my life as a pastor,

---

1. John Ralston Saul, *The Comeback* (Toronto: Penguin, 2014). 4.

2. Charles Taylor, *A Secular Age* (Harvard: Harvard University Belknap Press, 2007), 29.

seminary teacher, and consultant. In other words, I have spent forty-plus years witnessing up close a period of massive upending, decentering, and unraveling. What have we been doing?

Renewal and the Relational Revolution: The 1960s to Mid-1970s

> Christian people produce institutional forms in each century which are well adapted to the needs and occasions of the previous century. . . . [M]ore often than not change in the world around the churches is perceived but not acted upon. . . . Our generation seems to be perfecting the art of culture-criticism without perfecting the arts which would bring about radical institutional change.[3]

The 1960s blew the head off the sense of entitlement and power that characterized the churches and the North American establishment for generations. The churches' responses to these eruptions were varied. Some, looking to the social movements of the first half of the century and joining protest movements for civil rights and peace, were energized by a longing for justice and social transformation. They saw the church as part of a new vanguard remaking society.

By the late 1960s, however, the energies of the increasingly suburbanized Protestant denominations had shifted. The majority of these churches, Rip Van Winkle-like, were asleep to what was happening all about them. Their focus wasn't on social movements but the growth of their own congregations. In the spirit of the time, there were calls for radical change and a shift from "tradition" to mission,"[4] but a majority of these calls for change looked inward in the belief that if something (let's call it an X factor) could be fixed, then the churches would be relevant again. Varieties of books were published with their version of what the X was and how the church would recover by fixing it.

---

3. Kyle Haselden and Martin Marty, *What's Ahead for the Churches?* (New York: Sheed and Ward, 1964), 12.

4. See Joseph C. McLelland, *Toward a Radical Church* (Toronto: Ryerson Press, 1967).

Not surprisingly, a growing number of voices called for the renewal of the church: organizational renewal, program renewal, worship renewal, every kind of renewal. There were calls for renewed worship through the introduction of new styles of preaching and contemporary elements (bring the rock concert into the church; exchange guitars, drums, and praise songs for hymns and organs; reintroduce more ancient forms of liturgy). Charismatic renewals in Catholic and Protestant churches infused struggling churches with hope for a new Spirit-directed vitality. These calls for renewal were framed as a return to the ministry of the laity or the recovery of the five-fold ministry pattern from Ephesians 4 (apostles, prophets, pastors, teachers, and evangelists). They were based on the conviction that the churches were too clerical and out of touch with a broader understanding of discipleship.

Books streamed from publishing houses demanding reevaluation of the church and its purpose. Some demanded a new face for the church, others a radical transformation of structures or an end to the mainline church's complicity with "The Establishment." There were calls for the greening of the church, while others trusted that churches would become effective by taking a hard look at their purpose based on the New Testament.[5] Even in the 1970s there was a call for an emerging church that had rediscovered its true goals and developed new strategies to meet the culture.[6]

Many wrote about the "relational revolution,"[7] which promised to reconnect people's personal aspirations and needs with God's purposes. The movement took many forms; one of the more prominent was Faith at Work, which sought to connect people to their work life as a central part of Christian identity. For others this renewal involved applying new psychological insights to what the Bible meant by healing and wholeness. The layman Keith Miller—author of *The Taste of New Wine*, *The Second Touch*, and *The Habitation of the Dragon*—was successful at pointing

5. E. Stanley Jones, *The Reconstruction of the Church—On What Pattern?* (Nashville: Abingdon, 1970); David Watson, *I Believe in the Church: The Revolutionary Potential of the Family of God* (London: Hodder and Stoughton, 1978); and Michael Harper, *Cinderella with Amnesia* (Downers Grove, IL: InterVarsity Press, 1975).

6. Bruce Larson and Ralph Osborne, *The Emerging Church* (Waco, TX: Word, 1970).

7. See Bruce Larson, *The Relational Revolution* (Waco, TX: Word, 1976).

Christians toward the inner life of the self and integrating work life with faith.[8]

The small-group movement came to the fore as a key for connecting people beyond arid Sunday worship or formal committees. Paralleling the development of the Human Potential Movement, transpersonal psychology, and Maslow's hierarchy of needs, church renewal movements sought to create a greater sense of relationality, honesty, and intimacy. This period also witnessed a renewed focus on clinical pastoral education. Clergy trained in hospitals to be clinically formed caregivers, like counselors or therapists. The almost medical model gave credibility to pastoral leadership in an age quickly disposing of that imagination.

Taken together, these proposals were driven by a conviction that if you could bring together a mixture of a) the moods, music, and ethos of contemporary (that is, Baby Boomer) culture with b) the essential, Biblical form of the church, and c) invite the Holy Spirit to stir the mixture, then d) the churches would be fixed and could return to their previous status at the center of society.

This is a sampling of what was happening, not the writing of a history. I have not taken into account the impact of the Vietnam War and protests, with their calls for a fundamental transformation of society, but this energy had moved to the background by the mid-1970s.[9] Sociologist Gibson Winter explains why in his classic, *The Suburban Captivity of the Churches*.[10] After World War II, the Euro-tribal churches fled to the new suburbs. This massive demographic change (driven by class, race, and economics) meant that by the late 1970s the majority of the Euro-tribal churches—certainly the majority of their membership and energy—had relocated to the suburbs. These churches were shaped around an emergent

---

8. Also consider the counter-critique of this inward shift in the writings of social theorists like Philip Rieff, *The Triumph of the Therapeutic: Uses of Faith after Freud* (Chicago: University of Chicago Press, 1966 and 1978); Christopher Lasch in his early book, *The Culture of Narcissism* (New York: Norton, 1979); and much later, Robert Bellah, Richard Madsen, William M. Sullivan, Ann Swidler, and Steven M. Tipton, *Habits of the Heart: Individualism and Commitment in American Life* (New York: Harper and Row, 1985).

9. See William Stringfellow, *An Ethic for Christians and Other Aliens Living in a Strange Land* (Waco, TX: Word, 1976).

10. Gibson Winter, *The Suburban Captivity of the Churches* (New York: Doubleday, 1961).

generation of Baby Boomers, characterized by a strong desire for experience, self-expression, and self-actualization. In this world, the church primarily focused on renewing itself to take care of its members, expand its programs, and generally make itself more attractive to the suburban public.

Church Growth: The 1970s and 1980s

By the mid-1970s into the 1980s, some different voices began answering the call for renewal. One was the church growth movement, and another the congregational studies effort. In each case the response to an increasing unraveling was to focus on making congregations more effective.

Church growth began in the 1960s, oddly enough, with a misapplication of Donald McGavran's *The Bridges of God: A Study in the Strategy of Missions.*[11] McGavran had been a missionary in India, and his book studied people groups with massively distinct socio-cultural and religious differences. His insights were turned into techniques for making churches in homogenous, North American suburbs boom. This is also when such terms as "attractional" and "seeker sensitive" came into vogue, as churches applied the technologies of marketing and media to the cohort of Baby Boomers beginning to comprise a new majority.

Denominations, schools, and para-church organizations created bands of church growth consultants who fanned out across the continent with binder-driven workshops, training events, and assessment tools to diagnose how a church could move off its plateau to the next numerical level. Growing churches were studied (again with little reference to their socio-cultural-geographic-political-ethnic contexts) to determine best practices that could be universalized to work in any church, anywhere. This movement shaped the mostly white, Euro-tribal Protestant churches and the emerging conservative evangelical majority. Just master the binder, ignite members' spirituality, enlarge the sanctuary, fix the parking lot, or completely relocate to the crossroads where malls and housing developments

---

11. Donald McGavran, *Bridges of God: A Study in the Strategy of Missions* (Eugene, OR: Wipf and Stock, 1954 and 2005).

were about to break ground. Scripture was one more tool under-girding the movement's claims: Jesus' announcement of the coming kingdom of God was equated with the numerical expansion of sub-urban congregations.

This movement is driven by the conviction that shaped its title: make churches grow. The implicit reality was that churches had stopped growing, but leaders resisted the Spirit's work of disruption and dislocation.

The congregational studies trend took a different tack but remained focused on assessing the inner workings of a congregation in order to help them to become effective again. It applied social science to congregations in order to enhance congregational self-understanding and health.[12] Socio-cultural and ethnographic case studies of congregational processes focused on the inner dynamics of church life. This pastoral instinct, coupled with the growing status of the social sciences, drew people to what seemed like a promising and hopeful way of addressing the unraveling.

During this period, the Charismatic Movement gained momentum and entered mainstream church culture, becoming respectable in the middle-class, emerging Boomer churches. It represented a genuine desire to hear the Spirit, but that yearning was mostly co-opted by the culture of experience and self-development and never really grasped the dislocating work of the Spirit.

The Corporate Approach: 1980s and 1990s

By the latter part of the '80s and into the '90s, diverging social movements were proclaiming the crisis of Western culture, the unraveling of the Western imagination, and the coming of a "new age" (in the spirit of the 1960s musical *Hair*). In the midst of this new age, a majority of congregations in North America experienced an accelerated unraveling. Denominations could no longer deny the dislocations. As funds diminished and congregational figures plummeted, and as successive attempts at reenergizing, restructuring, or otherwise introducing big new visions failed, national and

---

12. See Jackson Carroll and Karl Dudley, *Handbook for Congregational Studies* (Nashville: Abingdon, 1986).

mid-level church offices struggled to adjust. The corporate denomination was coming to an abrupt end, and no one had much sense of what would take its place beyond efforts to restructure or reduce program and staff.

The hub-and-spoke model of denominational life, with its centralized, expert-driven hierarchies at national headquarters and regions, was coming undone. But the response to this dislocating work of the Spirit was a continued effort at tweaking the model, often borrowing from the realm of business and strategic planning. Lots of experts discussed the effectiveness of market-driven and seeker church models.

Eventually, church growth morphed into a different metaphor, borrowed from the growing popularity of the health movement. The basic idea for the church health movement was to discover indicators of health for a congregation. A dominant player in church health was Natural Church Development or NCD, which uses a survey to measure a congregation's "health" in eight areas: empowering leadership, gift-oriented ministry, passionate spirituality, functional structures, inspiring worship, holistic small groups, need-oriented evangelism, and loving relationships. NCD is driven by a desire to create healthy, vital, growing congregations. But these indicators are freighted with huge, unexpressed assumptions and values that never get addressed. Most of all, they reflect the standard default of turning within the church both to name characteristics of health *and* to seek strategies for fixing it. NCD is one of a long series of health-based responses that assume the proper diagnosis will lead to a clear prescription. Like a course of drugs, this set of techniques will cure what ails the churches.[13] It is as if the disciples, having been driven beyond Jerusalem by the disruptive Spirit, had focused on ways of making the Temple habitable again.

By the 1990s people were increasingly losing confidence in this continuing round of strategies and proposals. The talk turned to a post-denominational, even post-Christian, solution apart from renewal, growth, health, or market-driven seeker church models.

---

13. "Need-oriented evangelism," for example, is itself a method that leaves those of us in the church in control of outcomes as we determine and meet needs in others. This stance, despite its best intentions, turns the other into an object and we stay in control of our lives.

Another generation was entering the scene. Raised in the Boomer-driven culture but suspicious of it, these leaders were slowly beginning to question, analyze, and even deconstruct the established church life of the twentieth century. This generation had not grown up with flourishing churches at the center of the culture. They were not familiar with a time before the unraveling. The language of "exile" made less and less sense to them. The location of the churches in the 1990s was all they had known. These younger generations wanted to reshape the church for a new millennium.

Emerging and Joining God: 2000 to the Present

The emergent church is a major example of this effort to frame an ecclesiological response in the new millennium. The fact that this movement, which in the first years of this century seemed so vital, has all but disappeared, points to the frenetic search for solutions to the crisis of these churches. Emergent church was a broad coalition of younger leaders seeking to frame a "new kind of Christianity" with new forms and practices of church life that claimed to link with earlier forms of Christianity. As a loosely knit network—some stand-alones and some affiliated with Euro-tribal churches—the movement catalyzed a plethora of experiments in worship and structure. Leaders sponsored conferences and social media conversations in the hope of giving concrete expression to these new forms of church and the imagination behind them. Compared to the Baby Boomers' mega-church format, they went small and intimate. It was a movement energized (and eventually jaded) by the 1990s hope that a new period in human history was emerging.[14]

There is something to the notion of a new world emerging. Francis Fukuyama wrote in 1992 about *The End of History*, where he proposed the end of existing global political and economic structures as the prelude to a massive shift in human imagination and formation.[15] Writers like Phyllis Tickle and Brian McLaren took it further in the 2000s, as they set the malaise and unraveling of the churches

---

14. See for example the writing of Fritjof Capra and its popularization in such writings as Marilyn Fergerson's book *The Aquarian Conspiracy* (NY: Tarcher, 1981).

15. Francis Fukuyama, *The End of History and the Last Man* (New York: The Free Press, 1992).

into the frame of human emergence, the birth of a new world. The emergent church movement was a brave attempt to reimagine and reform churches with a focus on ancient practices and the use of social media. For a time, it produced an outpouring of hope and creativity among younger leaders. Like any movement it raised difficult questions about theology, established orthodoxies, ecclesiology, and the formation of community. But it has proved less than durable compared to the realities of everyday life and the established norms of Protestantism in North America.

Another movement of the new millennium was missional church. Formed in the 1990s as the Gospel and Our Culture Movement, the language of "missional" became the hot church word early in this century. With the publication of *Missional Church: A Vision for the Sending of the Church in North America*, Euro-tribal churches heard the call to reorient themselves toward their original missional vocation. Informed by the writing of Lesslie Newbigin, the missional conversation engaged leaders across a wide spectrum of theological convictions. Where culture wars had divided churches around issues of absolute truth, ethics, worship forms, and Christian practice, the missional movement seemed to bring these diverse perspectives together around a common desire to reframe the church's identity for God's mission. (I have written about this issue at some length in other books, and was one of the authors of *Missional Church*, so I admit a personal stake in the conversation.)[16]

The intent was to assist the churches in grasping that mission isn't just an element, program, or committee of the church, but its core identity. The word "missional," however, is now an adjectival modifier for practically everything congregations and denominations do. The basic theological and missiological motives of the movement were quickly redirected back into church questions, and the movement has widely been turned into a series of tactics for church renewal, growth, and health, despite its founders' best intentions.

Notice how quickly these fresh movements of hope and innovation turned back into fix-the-church initiatives. It is a testimony to the powerful ecclesiocentric defaults that shape the Euro-tribal

---

16. See Alan J. Roxburgh, *Missional: Joining God in the Neighborhood* (Grand Rapids, MI: Baker Books, 2011).

churches on this continent. The list of new initiatives can be extended—liquid church, sticky church, fresh expressions church, messy church, simple church, back-to-church Sunday—but they all hang on the conviction that the church is the center of the problem.

In particular, church planting has returned as a major emphasis. Denominations are hiring staff to direct church-planting initiatives for planting hundreds of new churches. Coalitions are springing up focused on training, nurturing, and producing church-planting movements. Too often this development represents an attempt to bypass the intransigent challenge of transforming existing congregations. The hope is that new churches will connect with the culture via more basic, grassroots styles of church less encumbered with denominational distinctives or the histories of existing congregations. No one will say it, but it seems clear that after more than half a century of trying to fix and renew existing congregations, we are getting weary with the lack of success. It's easier to start fresh than fix what exists. This is a misplaced assumption in the economy of God.

One potential bright light is new monasticism, which emerged at the beginning of the new millennium. Centered on communities of God's people sustained through practices of common living, this movement sought to break with the acquisition and accumulation of consumer, capitalist societies. New monastics seek to reengage with Christian practices such as hospitality, welcoming the stranger, living simply, and caring for the earth. Common life is shaped around the Daily Office or liturgical year, and those who participate demonstrate a growing commitment to the local. They want to live and be church in the neighborhood, to shape common life and witness in the places where they live with and for their community. They are not only creating new Christian communities; they are finding ways of being a new society. While small in number and living without fanfare, this movement is influencing Christians who sense the inadequacies of the actions summarized in this chapter.

There is an increasing recognition across the Euro-tribal churches that tactics, metrics, programs, demographics, health assessments, or strategies for institutional reorganization are not approximations of the Jesus movement the Spirit is inviting us into across our neighborhoods. New monasticism, along with counterparts like the Parish Collective and the slow church movement, are indicators that after more than fifty years of trying to fix the church, significant numbers of Christians are hearing the Spirit's call to journey in a different way.[17]

What Have We Done?

This chapter presented some snapshots and soundings across a fifty-year period. Without being exhaustive it has offered these images in response to the question, "What have we done to address the unraveling?" What we've seen can now be summarized as follows:

1. Up to the '60s, the Euro-tribal churches experienced a period of significant flourishing and saw themselves at or near the center of North American society.

2. Beginning in the mid-1960s that period came to an abrupt halt. The unraveling had begun and it produced increasing levels of anxiety. The churches engaged in more than fifty years of efforts at church growth, health, and renewal, all to get back to their normative location at the center of society.

3. God's disruptive, dislocating Spirit is continuing to call these churches on a different journey. After these fifty-plus years of unraveling, people might be ready to hear the Spirit's voice in fresh ways.

---

17. See Paul Sparks, Tim Søerens, and Dwight Friesen, *The New Parish: How Neighborhood Churches Are Transforming Mission, Discipleship and Community* (Downers Grove, IL: InterVarsity Press, 2014); and Christopher Smith and John Pattison, *Slow Church: Cultivating Community in the Patient Way of Jesus* (Downers Grove, IL: InterVarsity Press, 2014).

CHAPTER THREE

Four Misdirecting Narratives (or "Why Have We Done It?")

You know, Tillich, Christianity has no meaning for me whatsoever apart from the Church, but I sometimes feel as though the Church as it actually exists is the source of all my doubts and difficulties.

—J. H. Oldham (1959)[1]

Institutionally and ideologically, materially and morally, we need not have ended up where we are. Human decisions were made that did not have to be made, some of which turned out to be deeply consequential. Patterns were established, aspirations justified, expectations naturalized, desires influenced, and new behaviors normalized that need not have taken hold . . . not historical inevitabilities but rather the institutionalization and reinforcement of certain desires, values, decisions, and behaviors rather than others.

—Brad S. Gregory[2]

Attempts to address the unraveling described in the previous chapter came from a genuine desire to see congregations and denominations thrive as agents of God. But there is a set of underlying characteristics in these initiatives that misdirect their best intentions and most ardent prayers. This chapter describes those characteristics and convictions.

In the 1960s, as these churches entered this long unraveling, Thomas Kuhn wrote a book that gave people a language for

---

1. J. H. Oldham, *Life Is Commitment* (New York: Associated Press, 1959), 85.

2. Brad S. Gregory, *The Unintended Consequences of the Reformation* (Cambridge, MA: Belknap-Harvard Press, 2012), 12.

understanding the massive social shifts that had hit Western societies. One of those words was *paradigm*.[3] A paradigm is a belief system that lies deep inside us as a group or society, like the operating systems that hum inside our computers. Paradigms drive how we act and can be so deeply embedded in us as a community that we just assume our framing of the world is the true one.

The word *narrative* has something of the same connotation. It means the story that holds us as a group, determining how we see and explain our world. Another word I find useful is *default*. We default when we automatically revert to established patterns and habits. About a month ago, Jane rearranged the kitchen. The pots and pans were given a new home. I am still turning to their original home and getting annoyed that they're no longer there. Defaults drive our actions, because they allow us to automatically live inside an established story. What do the actions summarized in chapter two tell us about the underlying narratives or paradigms that have informed responses to the unraveling? In particular, I see four narratives driving the churches' actions:

1. Functional rationalism ("We have the technology; we can fix it.")
2. Management and control ("With the right management, we can guarantee success.")
3. Ecclesiocentrism ("If we can fix the church, all will be well.")
4. Clericalism ("We are the ordained; we must have the answers.")

This chapter describes each of these faulty narratives, on the way to understanding the option that could move us from a narrative of privation to one of abundance.

Functional Rationalism: "We have the technology; we can fix it."

Functional rationalism is a fancy way of saying we can design a technology to fix whatever we are facing. It has been at the heart of Western life for the last half-century. I remember watching *The Six Million Dollar Man* on TV with my kids. The main character,

---

3. Thomas Kuhn, *The Structure of Scientific Revolutions* (Chicago: University of Chicago Press, 1962).

Steve Austin, was a test pilot flying a small, manned rocket ship to the edge of the earth's atmosphere. Something went terribly wrong and the ship plummeted back to earth, landing in the desert. Austin was injured beyond repair. This seemingly hopeless situation wasn't hopeless because—and this was the mantra beginning every episode—"We have the technology, we can do it!" Indeed, Austin wasn't just fixed; thanks to bionic technology, he could run faster, jump higher, see further, and think better than any human ever had.

This was more than technology as a fix; it was technology as the key to transformation. *The Six Million Dollar Man* was the summation of one of the deepest, most entrenched narratives of our time: with the right amount of counting, analyzing, assessing, organizing, planning, and technology, we can name the problem and create the solution for every situation.

Mind you, I am far from anti-technology. Technology is a massive gift. Instrumental rationality, in particular, has been liberating to human life and advanced such things as medicine and communication. What I would argue is that a set of defaults has driven the Euro-tribal churches in their response to the great unraveling, and those defaults have everything to do with our self-determined power to calculate and develop the techniques to dissect, manipulate, and engineer desired outcomes.

With all this technology, who really needs God? Instead, there is among churches an overriding conviction that with the right techniques and methods it is possible to usher in the kingdom. This belief system runs in the background of all the surveys to determine how healthy your church is, all the reorganizational strategies, all the techniques for how to grow a church. Can God actually change reality? It seems we're not sure, so we hedge our bets with more studies, dashboards, and desperate proposals to renew, grow, or return the church to health.

Again, I don't mean to sound like a Luddite or like I'm dismissing the gift of technology or rationalism. But when these are generalized to meet the challenges before us as Euro-tribal Christians, then this rationality, like a colonizing parasite, determines our actions; it controls how we read the reality facing the Euro-tribal churches and reshapes biblical narratives to match our criteria. Philosopher Marshall McLuhan is famous for the aphorism, "First we shape the tools and then the tools shape us." It fits this situation. Instrumental rationality so deeply shapes the practices of our church and leaders that it determines how we read, interpret, and act on the Gospel and Christian tradition. Fundamentally, it provides us with the capacity to create solutions apart from the actions of God. It leaves us in control.

Our response in these instances is entirely understandable. When something precious unravels, our default is to try to fix it. Who would not? Recall the story of my granddaughter Maddie's Blanky, how it unraveled and her mom and grandma continually tried to fix it. This is what we've been doing with the churches for more than half a century. It will not work. Why? Because fixing is based on the assumption that the only thing necessary is some adjustment (better programs, improved liturgy, more genuine caring, *really* getting to know the needs of the community, and so on). Fixing isn't about a new imagination; it's improving what we're already doing. This is not where the Spirit is inviting us to journey.

Control and Management: "With the right management, we can guarantee success."

Another conviction at work in the responses we saw in the last chapter is that, with the management process, we are guaranteed control and predictability. The fixing language assumes leaders can stay in control of the agenda and manage outcomes. This question of control and management is nothing new; it is continually rehearsed in Scriptural accounts of the relationship between God and the Israelites.

Moses' encounter with God at the burning bush in Exodus 3 illustrates this tension as well as any passage could. Moses has been wandering around the desert looking after a few sheep for his father-in-law, when God makes himself known to our erstwhile patriarch:

> Then Moses said, "I must turn aside and look at this great sight, and see why the bush is not burned up." When the Lord saw that he had turned aside to see, God called to him out of the bush, "Moses, Moses!" And he said, "Here I am." Then he said, "Come no closer! Remove the sandals from your feet, for the place on which you are

standing is holy ground." He said further, "I am the God of your father, the God of Abraham, the God of Isaac, and the God of Jacob." And Moses hid his face, for he was afraid to look at God.

Then the Lord said, "I have observed the misery of my people who are in Egypt; I have heard their cry on account of their taskmasters. Indeed, I know their sufferings, and I have come down to deliver them from the Egyptians, and to bring them up out of that land to a good and broad land, a land flowing with milk and honey, to the country of the Canaanites, the Hittites, the Amorites, the Perizzites, the Hivites, and the Jebusites. The cry of the Israelites has now come to me; I have also seen how the Egyptians oppress them. So come, I will send you to Pharaoh to bring my people, the Israelites, out of Egypt." But Moses said to God, "Who am I that I should go to Pharaoh, and bring the Israelites out of Egypt?" He said, "I will be with you; and this shall be the sign for you that it is I who sent you: when you have brought the people out of Egypt, you shall worship God on this mountain."

But Moses said to God, "If I come to the Israelites and say to them, 'The God of your ancestors has sent me to you,' and they ask me, 'What is his name?' what shall I say to them?" God said to Moses, "I am who I am." He said further, "Thus you shall say to the Israelites, 'I am has sent me to you.'" God also said to Moses, "Thus you shall say to the Israelites, 'The Lord, the God of your ancestors, the God of Abraham, the God of Isaac, and the God of Jacob, has sent me to you':

This is my name forever, and this my title for all generations.

(Exodus 3:3–15)

Note how the pronouns reveal the issues of power and control occupying Moses' imagination. In verse 3 he states: "I will turn aside and see this great sight." God calls out of the bush and, again, Moses responds: "Here I am." The dialogue continues to revolve around the usage of this personal pronoun "I." It seems the writer is framing the story of Israel's future around the question, "Who is in control?" In other words, who is "managing" the outcomes and directions? Moses sees himself as the prime actor who chooses to make certain moves (as he did in Egypt, where he fought back against the soldiers who beat Israelites).

Then the Exodus writer shifts the tone and God's voice becomes primary. God creates a boundary, tells Moses not to come closer, and announces his own identity and intentions with a series of personal pronouns that put the lie to Moses' claims: "I am the God of your father, the God of Abraham, the God of Isaac, and the God of Jacob." "I have observed the misery of my people who are in Egypt." "I have heard their cry. . . ." "I have come down." "I will send you." The dynamic is not simply the announcement of God's decision to act. It addresses the question of who is the primary agent/actor.

Moses redirects the dialogue with a predictable question about himself: "Who am I that I should go to Pharaoh . . . ?", to which God responds, "I will be with you." After more negotiation, Moses makes a final request: "If I come to the Israelites and say to them, 'The God of your ancestors has sent me to you,' and they ask me, 'What is his name?' what shall I say to them?" This question isn't as simple as it might sound. When Moses asks for God's name, he's asking for the power of God's name so that he, Moses, can direct that power when he goes to Egypt. Moses was not venturing forth unless he was in control of God.

God responds: "I am who I am. . . . you shall say to the Israelites, 'I am has sent me to you.'" An ocean of ink has been spilled about this statement and its meaning. The point here is that the meaning to Moses is abundantly clear: "Moses, you cannot have control of my name. You will not go on this journey as the one who can manage and control the outcomes or who I am!"

This tug-of-war has characterized so much of churches' response to the unraveling. We say we trust God, but actions speak more loudly than confessions. In practice God is often not a factor except in terms of prayers for help. As one minister put it succinctly at a conference on church growth: "What's the matter with this program? It works!" This leader, like so many others, believes we can define a preferred future and develop actions to make that future happen. Parker Palmer describes such colonization this way:

> We are well-educated people who have been schooled in a way
> of knowing that treats the world as an object to be dissected
> and manipulated, a way of knowing that gives us power over the
> world. . . . I have used my knowledge to rearrange the world

to satisfy my drive for power, distorting and deranging life rather than loving it for the gift it is. . . . For many years I regarded thinking as a kind of board game in which we moved the pieces around until we have solved the problem, placing the pieces in patterns that allow us to "win."[4]

Ours is a world of calculation, control, and predictability. A conviction of God's agency in the world is displaced with actions empty of any sense of God's working.

Again, I promise that this is not a critique of good management. Organizations need to be well managed. The problem comes when the techniques and skills of management become the default solution to the churches' unraveling. We lose the capacity to hear the dislocating invitation of the Spirit. As one student told me, while describing the church to which he had been called:

First Church attendance and membership peaked around the time the current building was constructed in the '70s. Since then they've slowly declined. In recent years the church has attempted to reverse that decline by changing its polity, modifying worship styles, adding staff, exploring models of growth, and making many other programmatic changes. Leadership copied approaches that seemed effective in other places to implement a turnaround, while members of the congregation grew increasingly concerned about the state of the church. "Purpose driven" efforts were made to create "fully devoted followers of Christ" through new small groups, a revamped family ministry, and contemporary worship music. Some programs seemed to help attract new people but for the most part the trend of decline continued. Eventually efforts turned toward making First Church a "simple church" by pruning programs and turning the focus of the church outward.

Like any good business, churches create target audiences, define a type they will reach, implement generationally defined worship services, and design market-driven advertising to get "customers." The workbooks may begin with biblical framing, but then

---

4. Parker Palmer, *To Know as We Are Known* (San Francisco: Harper, 1993), 2–3.

it's back to the list of ten defining characteristics and how you can achieve them.

The basic flaw in this default is that we now live in a world where nothing is predictable. I recently received a web link to a denominational program on congregational vitality. The site offered a series of study guides with bullet-point lists of indicators for a vital congregation. There was another list of indicators for a missional church. I could not help but wonder, "Do we really believe that with indicator lists, programs and experts we can manage ourselves back to life?" We don't live in a world of such manageability and control. Practically everyone sitting in a pew on a Sunday morning, or attending a vision-planning evening, knows that the world where good management techniques could give us control of our future is gone. The key words today are agility and adaptability. Why do leaders still put so much faith in what we know to be limited?

Management is not the simple, neutral, natural word we might imagine. It is fraught with assumptions about control. In the modern narrative, *agency* becomes equated with *power*, and power, to a large extent, means the capacity to control and manipulate things, groups, or persons toward a set of determined outcomes. This, after all, is the hope imbedded in the call for such things as mission or vision statements. Adam Seligman put it this way: "[O]ur use of agency as power itself presupposes a certain model of human nature and action that it purports to explain . . . the individual as autonomous actor."[5]

One pictures a military leader planning and managing outcomes or establishing clear strategies to get things done. Or imagine the famous Panopticon. In the eighteenth century, British social theorist Jeremy Bentham designed the building so that a single observer could watch and control the movements of everyone without them knowing they were being watched. It represented the epitome of the drive to power through management and control.[6]

All this planning, strategizing, data gathering, and managing tells a true story about who we think is really in charge of this world. God's agency is secondary, functioning as a background resource to support our own management efforts.

5. Seligman, *Modernity's Wager*, 21.
6. Ibid.

Ecclesiocentrism: "If we can fix the church, all will be well."

The Protestant churches of the West are fundamentally ecclesiocentric: the church focuses on fixing the church in the conviction that the church is the central question to be addressed.

The word *missional* entered our vocabulary some twenty years ago, and it was originally an effort to point us back to God's mission as the primary force driving Christian life and community. Over time, missional has been completely identified with ecclesiology (or the study and theology of church); it has become an adjectival modifier for all kinds of proposals for making the church work again. Even when the hope was to reverse the tendency toward ecclesiocentricism, the power of that impulse was too entrenched for the Euro-tribal churches to resist.

Compounding this ecclesiocentrism is a diminution in robust theological dialogue around questions of God's agency and Gospel engagement with Western societies. A thin, unreflective montage of tactics for making churches "relevant" has displaced such dialogue. Until this ecclesiocentric deformation is addressed, we will continue with plans and strategies to fix, reform, renew, and restructure the church, without understanding these very moves are themselves symptoms of the fundamental problem.

It is to be expected that the churches' actions over the past fifty years would focus on fixing the church and getting the nature and identity of the church right.[7] Especially following the European reformations, the church was at the center of the culture and shaped the identity of emerging nation states and intellectual revolutions that would transform the West. As a result Christian imagination turned in on itself, and the greatest minds struggled over the nature and identity of the church. Leaders continually directed our attention inward, to automatically see everything from an ecclesiocentric perspective.

This is exacerbated whenever Christians define church primarily as a building or place within which the Word is rightly proclaimed, the sacraments rightly given, and discipline rightly administered. This definition effectively locates all of Christian identity inside an

---

7. See, for example, the debates about identity from the 1960s on, especially in the work of Hans Küng, *The Church* (New York: Doubleday Image, 1976).

ecclesiocentric frame. God is an agent largely within the spatial reality of a building or place where certain "holy" things occur, and God is represented by the ordained men and women set aside to carry out God's work.

This default imagination remains dominant, even though it depends on seeing the church as central to the social, economic, intellectual, and political structures of society. While this reality no longer exists (hence the "end of Christendom" conversations), we continue to carry within us a sense that the ecclesial questions are the central ones to be addressed. As a result, in the midst of massive dislocation and a whole new set of challenges and questions, most of our energies are still put to questions about making church work.

The unraveling will never be understood or addressed so long as we believe it is a question of fixing the church. We must follow missiologist Lesslie Newbigin's challenge and discern ways of joining with God in addressing the cries of increasing numbers of people caught in the nexus of destructive social narratives and a globalizing, urban capitalism run amok. More than twenty-five years ago Newbigin named the challenge for Christian life in the West with this question: What would be involved in a missionary encounter between the gospel and this whole way of perceiving, thinking, and living we call "modern western culture"?[8] We saw this question in the introduction, but this time I want to notice something else. See how Newbigin worded the question—it was not primarily about the church. He was not asking, first and foremost, what kind of church do we need? He was not asking what programs or methods or styles the churches needed. This was not because he was disinterested in the church. Right up to the time of his death, he was vitally involved in the life of local churches. For Newbigin the point of engagement is the interrelationship between the Gospel (and, therefore, what God is up to in the world) and the culture of the West. Church questions were secondary. Newbigin's focus was on the agency of God and, therefore, the relationship of the Gospel with Western culture.

Like Newbigin, I would never deny the necessity of believing, worshiping communities. I am simply convinced that we need to

---

8. Lesslie Newbigin, *Foolishness to the Greeks* (Grand Rapids, MI: Eerdmans, 1986), 1.

ask different questions. The deformation of Christian life cannot be addressed by continually asking church questions.[9]

Clericalism: "The ordained represent God; they must have the answers."

The fourth element characterizing practically all the initiatives described in chapter two is their overarching clergy-centeredness. If church is the center of Christian concern, the ordained, the clergy, are the primary agents of all that goes on *inside* the church. It is all well and good to declare that the work of the clergy is to prepare and send the people on God's mission in the world, but in action most clergy represent and incarnate a completely different narrative: the narrative of ecclesiocentrism.

The books on renewal, the proposals for a new kind of church, programs for growth or health, the social-science research on congregational life, the restructuring and reorganizing actions have mostly emanated from the ordained, a class of professionals whose orientation is by definition within the bounds of church life. This means the proposals for addressing the unraveling have come to a large degree from those formed in the ecclesiocentrism discussed above.

Two interactive dynamics, therefore, determine how these churches understand and engage their malaise. First, there is the default toward privileging expert and professional perspectives inside ecclesiocentric frameworks. The clergy are the ones who have been trained in matters of the church and God; they have professional degrees, so they're the experts and should know (better than others?) what to do. The functional result is seen in the initiatives addressing the unraveling of these churches from the 1960s forward. They're clergy-driven.

Second, this means the ordinary people of God have been socialized to assume they have neither the capacities nor the training to discern what God might be doing in the midst of the unraveling. The irony is that ordinary people—who have the perspectives the church desperately needs—have instead handed over the responsibility to clergy—who often cannot see beyond church enough to address what

9. See Daniel M. Bell Jr., *Liberation Theology after the End of History: The Refusal to Cease Suffering* (London: Routledge, 2001); and Graham Ward, *The Politics of Discipleship: Becoming Postmaterial Citizens* (Grand Rapids, MI: Baker Academic, 2009).

is facing the church! Clergy are colonized by ecclesiocentrism, in established churches and also in some of the new, emerging forms of church. So long as the questions remain about fixing the church, and the clergy are viewed as the key arbiters of that fix, little will change.

Clergy have been trained, ordained, hired, and paid by the church, so they naturally see themselves as responsible for addressing the unraveling. They are driven by the belief—and the external expectation—that they need to have the answers. Their titles imply it: Father, Mother, Priest, The Reverend. They have authority to shape people's fundamental interactions with community and with God, and to heal what ails God's people. Even when they know they don't know how, in my experience, most clergy feel this burden to fix. It does not help that the baptized increasingly default to the clergy for direction. Clergy-centrism is a deeply embedded default among us all.

As denominations and congregations continue to be de-centered and dislocated, clergy are increasingly disoriented and anxious. One clergy person explained the challenge and the opportunity to me in these words: "We keep acting as if we're in control and can manage our way out of all this disruptive change. How could we imagine ourselves being God's people in a time and place where we're not in control and can't manage the outcomes? What kind of system will we need to live into this reality?"

Despite years of theological training and the assumption that we are "spiritual" leaders, the clergy-centric initiatives of the past fifty years have been largely shaped from within the dominant narratives of modernity. Namely, they assume that with the right data and the right strategies, with the right restructuring or vision plan, with the right person at the helm, it is possible to manage the church from malaise into a new future. We are now in a land where these maps no longer apply to the geography.[10] The majority of people in North America are under fifty and have only inhabited life after the Euro-Protestant story. Even those younger generations who remain within the Euro-tribal churches are less and less able to connect with the dominant church narrative. And yet, with few exceptions, seminaries continue to train clergy to direct life and ethos for groups with a preexisting relationship to the Christian story. Without

---

10. See Alan J. Roxburgh, *Missional Map Making* (San Francisco: Jossey Bass, 2011).

interrupting this pattern, church leaders will probably continue proposing church-centered and clergy-driven solutions to the great unraveling. It is essentially the only world they know.

The Case for the Church

Each time I frame these proposals, I hear responses like, "It sounds like there is no place for the church" and "So you think the church doesn't really matter!" I am certain God is active in the church. God calls and forms us into communities of worship, learning, support, and discernment. For me, gathering as God's people around the Eucharist (Communion or Lord's Supper in many traditions) is a non-negotiable fact of Christian identity.

The point I am making is not an either/or claim about where God is to be found. It is a contextual claim about the Euro-tribal, Protestant churches and how the Spirit is calling them at this time. These churches have so turned in on themselves that they presume the church is the primary focus of their energy; they work on being attractional, on growing, on meeting needs and helping people, or on designing programs to send a segment of their members to serve outside their walls. What has happened through this long period of introversion and anxious search to fix the unraveling is that these churches, overall, have lost the capacity to discern the disruptive work of the Spirit beyond their circles. They have yet to be convinced that God's primary location is out ahead of the churches, and not only inside them.

The next chapter will look into the claim that God—and not church—is our first concern. But first, let me expand the summary at the end of chapter two to include this chapter's insights:

1. Until the 1960s, the Euro-tribal churches enjoyed a long period of success and dominion in North America and viewed themselves at or near the center of society.[11]

2. Beginning in the 1960s, that growth came to an abrupt halt for most so-called mainline churches and a period of unremitting

---

11. See Dwight Zscheile's *People of the Way: Renewing Episcopal Identity* (New York: Morehouse Publishing, 2012), especially his discussion of the "establishment" legacy of The Episcopal Church. This experience was also true, to some degree, for other Euro-tribal denominations in the first half of the twentieth century.

unraveling began. That dive has continued into the present, and it has produced a narrative of anxiety and scarcity that drives people to try to fix the churches and resume their post at the center of society. All of this has exacerbated a default fixation on the church, what we are calling the ecclesiocentric default.

3. The great unraveling is now a tsunami sweeping away this ecclesiocentric default. A different imagination is needed across North America, one that is no longer focused on ecclesiocentric questions but seeks to discern how we can go on a shared journey of discernment with the Spirit in the neighborhood.

CHAPTER FOUR

God at the Center (or "Who Is Really in Control?")

The members of the Task Force for Reimagining The Episcopal Church (TREC) believe that the Holy Spirit is calling our Church to participate in God's mission in a faithful and life-giving way in a changing world.

—Engaging God's Mission in the 21st Century: Final Report of the Task Force for Reimagining The Episcopal Church[1]

Being Church in the Neighborhood

I was in Edmonton, Alberta, when a long, hard winter suddenly turned, from one day to the next, into a warm spring. The sun shone brilliantly as the temperature shot into the 60s. It's the kind of radical transition that makes people do new things and see in a new way.

The same day, Ron Smith had an epiphany. Ron is part of a church community Karen Wilk developed in a neighborhood in Edmonton. Over supper, Ron and his wife told me about their life in the church until recently. They had belonged to churches in various cities and gotten used to the ritual of driving to church, serving on committees, and even going on mission trips. They had been very busy but rarely felt they were truly following and joining with Jesus in their whole lives. That shifted when they started to try out being church in the neighborhood.

Just that afternoon, Ron was on his way to the back deck with a beer to enjoy the warmth. Then he stopped, turned around, and headed toward the front door. He'd been getting to know people in

---

1. *Engaging God's Mission in the 21st Century: Final Report of the Task Force for Reimagining The Episcopal Church* (December 2014), 1. Available at *www.generalconvention.org/trecreport*.

his neighborhood and it was time to go deeper. Packing a hamper with beer and carrying some chairs, he headed for the front lawn. Within a half hour or so, a bunch of neighbors were enjoying cold beer and conversation. The gathering gave him a glimpse of what church could be.

This didn't just happen out of nowhere, but it also wasn't some carefully planned strategy for evangelism and mission. It was an experiment with a new practice—moving from the privacy of the back deck to the welcoming space of the front lawn. And it wasn't the work of a stereotypical young risk taker; Ron is recently retired. Yet, I was struck by the excitement and energy in his voice as he shared this experience.

Karen Wilk shares similar stories of the shift in her own vocation. She had been a key staff leader on the pastoral team of a large church for decades, running programs and training people in discipleship. Slowly, she discovered that she was detached from the people on her street and disconnected from her community. She started to change the patterns of her life, as she became more and more certain that Jesus was calling her to reenter her neighborhood and be with the people.

That hope has borne great fruit over the years. She has opened her home and welcomed others to live with her; she hosts a monthly Soup Night in her home and invites the neighborhood to gather to share food and life stories around the table. Karen has no trouble seeing God at work and sensing how the Spirit is forming something quite different from the church ministry she had maintained for so many years.

These kinds of stories are already cropping up across North America. The hand wringing about decline is being replaced with a conviction that God is up to something. Ordinary people in local contexts are discovering a different energy and hope as they test ways of joining with God in their neighborhoods. There is no pretense that those involved have it all worked out. There's lots of messiness and experimenting as people act and learn their way into a different imagination, and we will see in part II just what those actions could look like. In this moment, we will pay attention to the new imagination that makes those actions possible.

God Is in Control

We are witnessing a great transformation. At the core of this change is the deep conviction that God is the primary actor who is out ahead of us in the neighborhood. The huge challenge for the Euro-tribal churches is how we come to release our techniques, management, and desire to fix the church, and instead believe it is God who is acting out ahead of us, particularly in our neighborhoods.

At first glance the notion of joining with the God who is ahead of us in the neighborhood seems straightforward. In fact, there is some genuine reorientation involved. It means life with Jesus isn't primarily a private affair or even primarily a church-centered affair. It means we are committed to actively transforming our communities. It calls us away from ecclesiocentrism and church questions, and toward a whole set of disruptive questions about what God is up to and how we can join.[2] It calls us into the risky space of discerning where God is at work rather than depending on our own assessments of needs, which conveniently leave us in control of agendas and relationships.

Perhaps most painfully, a commitment to God's agency requires us to lay down our need to know ahead of time what this will mean for church forms and structures. If anything, churches will have to be willing to lay down control and go with Jesus into the local before they can faithfully discern what remaking the church will involve today. Participating in the mission of God has to come prior to knowing what the church will be.

There have always been prophets who have spoken and lived this conviction, but they have been hard for us to hear through our powerful ecclesiocentric defaults. We will have to pay closer attention to texts like Exodus 2:23–24: "In the course of time the king of Egypt died, and the children of Israel cried out because of their bondage, and their cry came before God, and God heard their groaning and remembered." In these stories, it is clear that God is acting and the call is to go with God beyond the sea.

---

2. This book is not focused on constructing a comprehensive ecclesiology or theology of how God acts in the world. For more on this topic—especially on the notion of a *theodrama* (the church is placed in a great drama where God is the primary Actor)—see Hans Urs von Balthasar, *Theo-Drama: Theological Dramatic Theory*, vols. I–V, trans. Graham Harrison (San Francisco: Ignatius Press, 1988–1998); and Nicholas M. Healy, *Church, World and the Christian Life: Practical-Prophetic Ecclesiology* (Cambridge, UK: Cambridge University Press, 2000).

Some illustrations may help to fill in this picture. Just as we asked what these churches had been doing over the past fifty or so years to tease out underlying assumptions, we can look at the Biblical narratives for examples of what God has been up to. It is in God's *doing* that we see how God is the active agent; God's action also tells us where we will find a new direction and practices for the churches.

I. Exodus 2:23–3:15: What is God doing?

We saw the story of Moses at the burning bush in the introduction and again in chapter three, but I return to it here as an example of the narrative of God's deliverance. At first glance Moses seems to be its subject. In fact, God is the primary actor. The narrative is about a God who acts in the world in a specific way, toward and on behalf of a particular people. The people themselves were not so special; they were a group of slaves who had escaped an empire that declared them disposable. They were without power or a future, *but they were precious to God*. It is God who remembers and God who acts. God is in control.

God is The One who hears their cry and comes down to them. This is the God of Abraham, the God of Isaac, the God of Jacob, the God who acts in the concrete experience of a people who no longer know who they are. This God acts to reshape the world, with and among totally ordinary people who have been deemed of no value. Moses'—and the churches'—vocation is to participate in this primary drama of God's acting.

Exodus suggests exactly where we discern the practices for joining with God: on the way with real people, as we participate in life in the places where God is acting out ahead of us. The practices are not first learned inside church programs and then applied to people. On the contrary, they are discovered in our neighborhoods. This is where we must work out the questions of how to reweave the fabric of social and communal life, as God intends.

II. Ezekiel 1:1–28 and 37:1–14: Where is God to be found?

The prophet Ezekiel struggled with the temple's decline, and initially he assumed it was the people's fault. They had failed to set the temple in its rightful place, and if they could just return, all would be well.

Then he finds himself far from the temple, on the banks of the River Chebar where exiles from Tel-abib have gathered (1:1). Often in Biblical narratives, you find outsiders and unexpected wisdom near brooks, watering places, and wells. This is where God meets Ezekiel and grants him many visions.

In his first dream, he sees a series of wheels spinning in different directions, each with different colors and textures. In these wheels are human-like creatures, each with four faces turning in every direction. I wonder if the dream is God inviting the young temple prophet into a new way of seeing. In particular, God seems to be telling Ezekiel that God has a new set of wheels (playing loosely with the text), and that God is moving beyond the temple.

Later, the Spirit carries Ezekiel to a whole other place, a valley. Here he has the infamous vision of the valley of dry bones (37:1–14). The dream is harsh and jarring, but also full of hope. Peering into this valley of the dry bones, most people would be inconsolable. But the Spirit blows over the valley and the dry bones are brought to life. The point is clear: God calls things, people, and situations back to life. Would Ezekiel have seen this reality back at the temple? We will never know.

This book proposes that the Spirit is acting in a similar way today toward the Euro-tribal churches. The Spirit has been propelling us into places we cannot manage or control.[3] Our unraveled state is not punishment; it is the gift that forces us to learn to ask God-centered questions, to deny "modernity's wager" and admit that life cannot be lived well without any practical reference to the agency of God. The Spirit is calling us into a new imagination.

A Missionary God

Over almost two decades the missional conversation has argued that mission is the result, first, of God's initiative. It is rooted in God's purposes to restore and heal creation.[5] Further, mission is the "central

---

3. This does not mean the Spirit caused everything that took place. Rather, in the midst of much disruption and change, the Spirit has been calling but this call has been mostly missed.

4. See Darrell Guder's introduction to *Missional Church: A Vision for the Sending of the Church in North America* (Grand Rapids, MI: Eerdmans, 1998). For a fuller discussion of the missional conversation and God's agency, see Craig Van Gelder and Dwight J. Zscheile, *The Missional Church in Perspective* (Grand Rapids, MI: Baker, 2011).

biblical theme describing the purposes of God in human history."[5] As Craig Van Gelder and Dwight Zscheile have noted, God's mission in the world is related to the reign, or the kingdom, of God. This means the work of God is larger than the mission of the church, although the church is directly involved in the reign of God.

God is a missionary God, or as Van Gelder and Zscheile put it, God is a *sending* God. This is most clearly seen in the Incarnation, when God sent God's son for the life of the world. Most theologians would agree with this formulation, but Van Gelder and Zscheile extend and enrich it by introducing the notion of *participation*. The revelation of God in Jesus Christ means that God is not only the one who sends, but God is the one who, first and foremost, participates in the world.[6] God's sending can only be understood when paired with God's participation in God's own mission.

Important elements for the church come to the fore when we understand God as both sending *and* participating.

1. The missionary God who sends and participates in the world also sends the church into the world. The church is a living embodiment of this missionary God's identity and intention. This means everything the congregation does is shaped by a missionary commitment to the local context.

2. In our North American setting, the church is sent to engage and participate in our postmodern, post-Christendom, globalized contexts.

3. The church's internal life focuses on every believer living as a disciple engaging in mission. Worship, teaching, spiritual practice, fellowship—all are to prepare and send people to participate fully in God's mission.[7]

4. If the church is not the primary actor, but God is, then we have to assume God is already ahead of us. The church embodies and participates in what God is already doing. The questions, "What is God doing?" and "Where is God doing it?" now have to form the practices of the church. The church cannot know how to

---

5. Guder, *Missional Church*, 4..

6. Van Gelder and Zscheile, *The Missional Church in Perspective*, 106–11.

7. Ibid., 4.

embody the life of God unless it is alert to what God is already up to and participating with God in the specificity of its context.

5. The church's primary work is to listen for what God is already up to. Its life should be marked by listening, watching, entering, and participating in the life of the neighborhoods where God's people live in the ordinary and everyday, rather as Jesus did. "The Word came and dwelled (or 'pitched his tent') among us . . ." (John 1:14).

In the more recent Western tradition (particularly in missionary movements that accompanied colonization[8]), leaders tended to emphasize the *sending* function, especially the sending of the church as the primary active agent in mission. Everyone paid attention to what the church was doing *on behalf of* God and *for* the world. Following this thread, the church was sent to do the work of the church; the church went to reproduce itself in all kinds of places, including creating replicas of Euro-tribal church buildings wherever it went. Mission was, thus, largely ecclesiocentric.

The notion of participation shifts all this. What the church does is discern how and where it is called to participate *with* God in the world. Participation with God reframes agency from the church and back to God. The church comes to know its concrete identity through the act of discerning and participating, not the other way around.

Theologians have agreed for some time that the church could not be the starting point of mission.[9] Unfortunately this theological conviction failed to engage the actual life of the denominations and therefore did not significantly change their fundamental ecclesiocentrism. The kickoff book for the current missional conversation, *Missional Church*, illustrates this.[10] As one of the contributors, I know we sought to frame a robust theology of the mission of God (*missio dei*), but we were still operating from an ecclesiocentric base. The ensuing missional literature has done more of the same. Most do

---

8. See Willie James Jennings, *The Christian Imagination: Theology and the Origins of Race* (New Haven, CT: Yale University Press, 2010).

9. Van Gelder and Zscheile, *The Missional Church in Perspective*, 27.

10. Guder, *Missional Church*.

not begin from a point of asking the ways in which God is entering and participating in the everyday and local; they seek to frame some understanding of what it means to be the church and on that basis argue for a missional ecclesiology.

I believe the way forward is not just right thinking and right theology. We have to frame our lives around questions about God's actions in our neighborhoods and how to join with God in these places. The church's vocation is known only as an answer to this question: "What does it look like for us to go on a journey together in discerning what the Spirit is up to ahead of us in our neighborhoods?"

Taking the New Narrative Seriously

The Episcopal Church is one denomination attempting to grasp this changed imagination. In the summer of 2012, the church's leaders commissioned a task force to reimagine its structures, governance, and practices—no small order. The report they submitted in December 2014 serves as a tool for teaching and leading the church in this time, so I will quote it now at some length:

> The Church began as a movement, not an institution. Early Christians developed organization and structure as a necessary way to preserve, support, and spread the Jesus movement. The Book of Acts describes this as an exciting and dynamic process of experimentation, discernment, and discovery.
>
> The movement always precedes the institution, and practice always precedes structure. For this reason, we believe the most important thing we can do together in this moment is return to three basic practices that helped to animate the early Christian movement. We believe that, rather than an anxious focus on how to preserve our institution, a joyful focus on the basic practices of the movement will hold the real key for moving us into God's future. As in the past, the new future of The Episcopal Church will emerge from a focus on adapting and renewing the movement's basic practices in our own various local contexts while adapting the current structures to enable and even encourage this movement to catch on.

For a church accustomed to expecting people to find it and join its established life, this story from Luke's Gospel calls us to simple yet transformational practices that the church at every level must embrace today:

> Follow Jesus together. . . .
> Into the neighborhood. . . .
> Travel lightly. . . .[11]

This is an exciting and imaginative invitation. The Episcopal Church, like few other Euro-tribal churches, has begun to grasp what is at stake in responding to the Spirit's invitation to stop the "fixing" defaults and join the God who is ahead of us. Clearly this does not imply the end of once-dominant European churches. If they are to thrive, they will need to reimagine their identity and role. This will require them to reengage with the stories of their beginnings and understand how they can act apart from the ecclesiocentric defaults that have shaped their lives for decades or more.

These defaults are deep. They don't go away because a group has framed a prescient, imaginative invitation. How do we move past defaults that have been in place through most of the last century? What practices would help congregations and church-wide bodies to truly join up with God, to remake church, and ultimately to take their part in transforming communities so they reflect the reign of God? Part II outlines the shape of such a journey.

---

11. *Engaging God's Mission in the 21st Century: Final Report of the Task Force for Reimagining The Episcopal Church*, 2–3. Available at *www.generalconvention.org/trecreport*.

PART II

There is a great story happening. It has been invisible to most of us because we have been shaped by two or more generations of the ecclesiocentric drive to fix the church and make it work again. But God is up to something else, shaping a new direction across North America. I now want to turn to the question of how we can start to see that story for ourselves and how our congregations can join Jesus in this movement into our neighborhoods.

Congregations are traveling together into a new land, and the next several chapters explore a set of practices for how this can happen. Let there be no illusions around what it will take. There is hard work ahead and roadblocks to be encountered, some of which we will discuss. Changing our minds about what is important and learning new practices (for example, from *doing for* to *being with*) is a disorienting journey that takes courage and persistence. We also need some basic convictions that will carry us along roads that, initially, will seem strange. These convictions are as follows:

1. God is ahead of us in our neighborhoods, calling us to join.
2. God is present in the people who comprise our congregations, and the Spirit is present in their lives and actively inviting them on this journey.
3. God's ordinary people can listen to and hear God through one another as they dwell in the Word of God.

4. Leaders cultivate spaces for listening to the Spirit in life together.

5. A primary work of the ordained is cultivating a people of prayer, who collectively discern the Spirit in the vocation of prayer. The leader must lay down the anxious need to fix the church and make it work again.

6. An ordained leader cannot lead without doing, himself or herself, what the baptized are called to do.

These convictions help to counter the ecclesiocentric, clergy-centric narrative that has shaped life for the Euro-tribal churches.

With these foundations in mind, we can take the next step on this journey. It's time to practice.

CHAPTER FIVE

Practicing the Journey

Why practices? A big part of the answer to the question "How can we shift to a new narrative?" and specifically "How can a congregation go on this journey?" is found in the language of *practices*. Practices are shared actions that, when taken together, weave a way of life amongst a people.

A simple example is the recitation of the Lord's Prayer. A number of years ago I was wrestling with frustration toward someone, to the extent that it was affecting my attitude toward this person and others around him. A fellow Christian named John finally asked what I was doing about it. When I had no good answer, John challenged me to a regular practice of saying the Lord's Prayer three times a day. After several months the words came to me almost like breathing; they were such a natural part of me.

Each time I got to the line "forgive us our trespasses as we forgive those who trespass against us," I was confronted by my attitude. Eventually a change set in; the anger dissipated and I could bless the person who had so angered me. Several of my friends continue to regularly ask me how I am doing with the Lord's Prayer, as a gentle check in. Practices like this shape us communally into the ways of God.

Practices aren't just feelings, emotions, or sensitive, caring thoughts. They are routinized actions shaping our lives in a certain direction. Followers of Jesus by the mid-point of the first century were identified as "people of the Way"—this meant they were those who practiced the ways of Jesus. Like them, we are shaped into a particular way of life through the practices we determine to be important. As we take them on, they become a part of the rhythm of our lives; they get, as it were, into our ligaments, bones, muscle, nerves, and skin. They *embody* who we are together.

Practices build into our life together common habits, attitudes, and actions that orient us in a particular direction or way of life. They weave us into a life together. For example, several generations of my family gather for a common meal every weeknight, no matter what any particular member of the household is doing. Around the table we have common times for conversation and interaction. This practice has become an essential way for us to be more than a collection of people inhabiting the same space.

Weekly worship is another transformative social practice. It has been a core Christian practice since the beginning. Collectively, we've acknowledged that without this practice we cannot be who we confess we are: a people formed together by Jesus around the table. I don't know anyone who would support the claim that an individual can just worship alone. We believe there is something essential about coming together to practice being followers of Jesus, and even if we engage a practice alone, we do it with the awareness that others share the practice in another place but in the same Spirit. Practices are patterns of communal action that open up the presence of God and make God known among us.

Practices allow us to craft together a common life congruent with what we desire as God's people. In the context of this book our desire is to be a people who move in two directions at the same time. First, we desire to be released from ecclesiocentric defaults, from our obsession with fixing the church and making it work, from our focus on ourselves as the main actors and instead toward God as the chief actor. Second, we desire to be a people shaped by the way of Jesus who go lightly into our neighborhoods to discern and join with what God is already doing ahead of us. What, then, are the practices that move us in this direction and shape us into this people?

Gospel Foundations for Practice

There is no better place to start than with the gospel and the three broad practices summarized in the Task Force for Reimagining The Episcopal Church report we saw toward the close of chapter four. We begin with Luke 10:1–12:

After this the Lord appointed seventy others and sent them on ahead of him in pairs to every town and place where he himself intended to go. He said to them, "The harvest is plentiful, but the laborers are few; therefore ask the Lord of the harvest to send out laborers into his harvest. Go on your way. See, I am sending you out like lambs into the midst of wolves. Carry no purse, no bag, no sandals; and greet no one on the road.

"Whatever house you enter, first say, 'Peace to this house!' And if anyone is there who shares in peace, your peace will rest on that person; but if not, it will return to you. Remain in the same house, eating and drinking whatever they provide, for the laborer deserves to be paid. Do not move about from house to house.

"Whenever you enter a town and its people welcome you, eat what is set before you; cure the sick who are there, and say to them, 'The kingdom of God has come near to you.' But whenever you enter a town and they do not welcome you, go out into its streets and say, 'Even the dust of your town that clings to our feet, we wipe off in protest against you. Yet know this: the kingdom of God has come near.' I tell you, on that day it will be more tolerable for Sodom than for that town."

The sending in Luke 10 isn't about becoming social workers or fixing people's needs; the instructions leave them few means by which to help people or meet needs. The seventy are sent to embody and announce God's reconciling, healing future in neighborhoods. They are agents of God's actions, and so they take nothing with them, not unlike the Israelites sent into the desert.

The practices involved in this sending are critical to discerning what it means to join with God in our neighborhoods. The seventy are sent to practice dependence on the hospitality of the neighbor, as Israel was dependent on the hospitality of God in the desert. They were not to go as those in control. They had to discern what the Spirit was doing. The practices they learned involved dwelling, working, eating, listening, and healing with and among the people of these towns.

The locale of God's activity is clear: in towns, in homes, around tables, in the fields at work, in the meeting places of the everyday life of ordinary people. In other words, in the neighbor-hood. These practices are not formed from within preconceived church categories but out in the villages and among their people—again, as in the older Exodus tradition, they are formed out on the way, in the desert.

This does not make the church irrelevant, but it is a different way for existing churches to imagine themselves. Choosing not to begin with church questions, to let go of the prior need to fix the church, is counterintuitive but necessary to rediscover our vocation. It's not possible to become like the seventy in Luke by trying *first* to fix ourselves and *then* creating plans to engage our communities. It's impossible to know either the shapes congregations need to take or the structures that will best serve until we join with the One who is out ahead of us. It will be in the returning and reflecting together on what we are discerning that we will understand the shapes, forms, and structures our "new parishes"[1] need to take.

It's important to reemphasize these last sentences. People mis-understand what I am saying if they presume the church is no longer important or the practices of its inner life are irrelevant. Nothing could be further from the truth. What we are acknowledging is the present situation of the Euro-tribal churches and how they will dis-cover fresh ways in which their traditions, liturgies, and forms of dis-cipleship can become vital means for participating in God's mission in our contexts.

This is why The Episcopal Church report is so timely; it takes the Luke text and proposes three practices for congregations seeking to join God:

> **Follow Jesus together.** The Episcopal Church's identity is rooted in Jesus and his Way. The renewal of our Church will come only through discerning the shape of that Way and practicing it together in the power of the Spirit. Christianity is an embodied way of life, not just an institution or set of ideas. The Episcopal Church has a distinct and rich heritage of interpreting and expressing Jesus' Way. Every local church and every Episcopalian must be called to follow Jesus more deeply.

---

1. See Sparks et al., *The New Parish*.

Into the neighborhood. Jesus sends us together into the places where ordinary life unfolds. We are sent to testify to God's reign as we form and restore community by sharing in God's peacemaking and healing. This begins with deep listening to neighbors, relying upon their hospitality rather than expecting them to find us on our terms. In today's increasingly diverse world, we must learn how to bear witness to, and receive from, those of different cultures, faiths, and beliefs, "eating what is set before us." For many churches now disconnected from neighbors, this will mean attempting small experiments in sharing God's peace as we learn how to form Christian community and witness with those neighbors.

Travel lightly. Jesus sends us out empty-handed so that we might rely upon God's abundance, which sometimes comes to us through the hospitality of our neighbors. We must hold inherited structures loosely as we make space for alternative patterns of organizing our life together. We must discern what of our traditions is life-giving and what unduly weighs us down. Traveling lightly means going in vulnerably, risking being changed by God and our neighbors.

The three elements of following Jesus together, into the neighborhood, and traveling lightly frame the ways a congregation can depart the ecclesiocentric defaults and join God. God is ahead of God's people, dwelling, acting in concrete, everyday places. This is where we must practice together until we learn how at last to address the questions of being God's church.

Five Practices for the Journey

The following five practices are based on Jesus' instructions in Luke 10:1–12 and on my and my colleagues' experience with hundreds of congregations and leaders experimenting with how to go on this journey together. These practices are intended to be as simple and concrete as possible. They are intentionally designed as a set of steps because this is how most of us best learn new practices. While extremely simple, they invite a significant level of change in congregational habits. These are the five practices:

1. **Listening:** Attending to God, one another, and our neighborhoods
2. **Discerning:** Discovering where the Spirit is inviting us to join with God in our neighborhoods
3. **Testing:** Engaging simple actions to join with God in the neighborhood
4. **Reflection:** Gathering to ask, What did we do? What are we learning? Where did we see God at work?
5. **Deciding:** Determining what are the new ways we will now join with God in the neighborhood

As you get set to start the journey, keep these points in mind:

- The whole journey begins small and without a lot of fanfare, so that people can practice new practices without being in the spotlight.
- The journey should occur parallel to the normal programs, events, and rhythms of congregation life, not in their place. In other words, several things are happening simultaneously. All who are interested may participate in the listening conversations and Dwelling in the Word (detailed in the next chapter). Meanwhile, a small group of members enters into the discerning and experimenting practices to try going lightly in the way of Jesus into the neighborhood. It is okay that most people in the congregation will stand on the sidelines of the latter steps, gently observing. Most people learn new habits by watching others do them first.
- The journey through the first four practices takes eighteen to twenty months. At that point it is essential to invite the congregation to decide whether and how to repeat the cycle.

This is the deliberate journey for a congregation to shift its imagination and energy. These practices gently and gradually invite people into asking new questions and primarily seeking God's activity, all by journeying into their neighborhoods and reflecting on what they have been doing. Little by little, as the cycle repeats, more people get involved in joining the way of Jesus in their neighborhoods. Little by little, people slowly act their way into a way of life. You are not creating a program but introducing new practices, with the hope that they will become the way of life for more and more people in the congregation. As congregations learn how to go on this journey, they will discover a way out of their unraveling and in so doing become very different kinds of congregations.

Be warned this is a long and difficult journey. None of us change our habits easily or quickly. I hope the stories and practical accounts I will provide help to convince you that I understand this is no easy journey. But it is the journey onto which the Spirit is inviting us and, as such, it is worth everything.

There's nothing more energizing than joining with what God is doing. There is no better news for so many of our Euro-tribal churches than the good news that we don't need to stay in the place of loss and anxiety. We are being called onto this amazing adventure because the place where God transforms the world is in our own neighborhoods. And the way God is doing that is in the way of Jesus, the Luke 10 way.

CHAPTER SIX

Practice 1—Listening

Jesus' instructions in Luke 10 have to do with entering, receiving hospitality, and dwelling with the other. The practice at the heart of these activities is *listening*. As the journey starts, a congregation cultivates this practice.

While it sounds easy, the listening described here invites a dramatic change in congregational habits and attitudes. Consider this story:

> Jim and Ann have joined with a diverse group of people in the Los Angeles area to become a neighborhood congregation. Some in the group know each other, others are new. They're all drawn by a common desire to discern the ways God is ahead of them in the neighborhood. They know it won't be a matter of creating a program or even "studying" or "reading" the community, but practicing a way of listening. They are convinced that if they learn to listen to the Spirit, their eyes will open to what God is doing in their community, much like the story in which Jesus touched the eyes of the blind man.
>
> At their initial gatherings they share this desire and talk about how they might go about this listening. People admit how often we take our communities for granted, assuming we know all about the place we drive in and out of and call home. It is so easy to be asleep to one's own community, even to the people in our own homes and workplaces. The group, recognizing these realities, desired to learn how to "wake up" to their neighborhoods.[1]

---

1. See Clemens Sedmak, *Doing Local Theology: A Guide for Artisans of a New Humanity* (Maryknoll, NY: Orbis, 2002), 1–5.

The thirty or so people in this local church range from children in middle school to some in their mid-sixties. They decide that one way to "wake up" to the neighborhood is to begin with themselves. They will practice listening to one another and then see what they can learn about listening to God in the neighborhood.

They want to increase their comfort and capacity in sharing stories with one another, what they describe as giving "testimony."[2] They devise simple practices for use in the rhythm of their regular gatherings. This might mean gathering around a meal table and asking, "Where have you experienced God in your life this week?" Children and adults share their stories of such experiences. As people share, others listen attentively, asking questions that deepen the speakers' sense of being heard.

This practice starts to shape what they share with one another as they gather. It shapes their conversations about their week and fosters the expectation that God is present in their everyday experiences. Somewhere in the rhythm of listening and sharing, the group recites the Lord's Prayer together—a simple, known practice that continues to deepen their listening to God with each other.

There are many levels to this story of a community awakening to the practice of listening and, in that listening, deepening their awareness of how God is already present among them. In this weekly rhythm around tables they're learning to how to become an attentive and expectant people.

Congregations and neighborhoods have lost much of this capacity for listening with one another.[3] In most congregations, listening is directed either toward the front (the altar or the pulpit), where we've ritualized our relationships to the Holy; or to the head of the table (as in committee meetings), where we've formalized relationships

2. Note: The language of "testimony" might not fit well in some traditions. What's important is not the word as much as the reasons for the choice. They wanted to create a space where they grew in their comfort and capacities to listen to God as they listened to one another's stories.

3. See George Monbiot, "The Age of Loneliness Is Killing Us" in *The Guardian* (October 14, 2014); and Marc J. Dunkelman, *The Vanishing Neighbor* (New York: W. W. Norton, 2014).

around agendas and tasks. We've lost the practice of listening to one another outside of these structured interactions.

Recently, I had supper with a group of clergy students. I asked questions like, how did they decide to become ministers, how did they choose this seminary, how did they meet their spouse. The response was stunning. A few simple questions, some attentive listening, and the stories poured out. Eventually, having had a long teaching day, I confessed my need for sleep. But their response tells me we're starved for such moments. Congregations are as absent of this listening as any other place. The challenge in the journey of going lightly into our neighborhoods to listen for God is cultivating a congregational life where we do this with one another. Listening with our neighborhoods calls for congregations that practice listening with each other.

Listening is about giving attention to someone other than oneself. It invites me beyond the safety of formal roles or programmed expectations, and into a space where I hear your story as a critical part of what God is doing in the world. I recently sat with a group of leaders as they explained why the church was so connected with its neighbors and why people seemed so committed to this congregation. Kevin said, "Everyone knows that their story is part of who we are." Then Meg spoke the words I will never forget: "They feel seen," she said. I was stunned. The Spirit opened me to the life of that congregation in ways a whole book could not capture. Imagine being able to say about one's congregation: "It's a place where people feel seen." Imagine being Jesus' presence in the neighborhood, where people describe feeling this way in relation to your congregation. *This* is following Jesus together into the neighborhood.

Our congregations are too much akin to Lazarus, whose bindings are still tightly wrapped about his body, so that no one can actually see him. We do not see each other. Listening is a way of unbinding one another, inviting us to forget ourselves and set aside the need to provide solutions or answers or to cover our ignorance or vulnerability. We practice laying down the need to be heard, and instead practice hearing. Specifically, we are listening to one another, listening to God, and listening to the neighbor.

Listening to One Another: Sharing Stories

Practices need lots of practice. So we want to find multiple moments and opportunities in our congregations—formal and informal—to practice sharing our stories with one another. No organizational, structural, or programmatic changes are required. Sometimes, Appreciative Inquiry questions can help people to practice sharing their stories.[4] Great conversations can begin around questions like: "Can you share a story about the first time you came to this congregation?" "Do you remember first moving into your neighborhood? What was it like?" "What have been some of the most life-giving experiences for you in this church?" "When have you most experienced the presence of God in this congregation?"

In regular meetings or groups, you can experiment by posing a simple question each time you come together, such as, "Where might you have seen God at work this week?" At first, people get a little rattled by the question. They're not used to this kind of talk in church. We have to develop each other's capacity by gently inviting people to awaken to God's activity in their life. Ask the question with an open-ended quality. The language "Where *might* . . . ?" provides some tentativeness and suggests we aren't going to be certain but we can test and see.

Be ready, because unexpected people will often share stories in unexpected ways. Initially, there might be brief moments where someone offers a tentative observation. ("Just yesterday I was in the store and met M. We started talking and I had the sense that God was . . .") As people share stories with each other, they discover that someone else has experienced God in the midst. After a time, this capacity to practice listening with one another in a new way grows and this experience of naming God's presence in one another takes hold.

People don't need to feel there has been some momentous shift in program or worship life. They only need to begin simply and in small ways. As people share a bit of their story and/or where they have seen God at work, the energy and expectation of the group

---

4. There are lots of resources for introducing Appreciative Inquiry. See Mark Lau Branson's *Memories, Hopes and Conversations: Appreciative Inquiry and Congregational Change* (Durham, NC: Alban Institute, 2009).

grows. People become eager and hungry for this part of a meeting, and then you can build on these initial conversations.[5] In this beginners' practice, we are inviting congregations to wake up to their own stories of how God is already present in their life together.

Listening to God: Dwelling in the Word Together

A big part of going lightly into our neighborhood in the way of Jesus is discerning God's activity, which requires that we practice listening to what God might be doing. This happens as we learn to listen to one another's stories. Another primary way to listen for God's activity is through Scripture. The best practice I know for this listening—the one we use frequently via The Missional Network—is called Dwelling in the Word.[6] It's a way of letting God address us through Scripture, rather than using Scripture only as a tool for imparting new information or confirming existing beliefs. Dwelling in the Word invites the Holy Spirit to enliven a biblical text among us, so that we become aware of and responsive to what God is doing. This is a practice of listening to God through the text and through one another. Wherever we have introduced this practice, people report how life-giving it is.

Scripture has become inaccessible to most in our congregations who view it as the domain of the ordained or professional. Dwelling, on the other hand, is the work of the people. It is not so much a technique as it is learning to hear God together. It is a practice for discovering how to listen to God in our own voices and contexts. For some, it sounds arrogant to assume any of us could determine what God is up to. We may have in our hearts the Scripture, "My ways are not your ways, nor my thoughts your thoughts, says the Lord" (Isaiah 55:8). Of course, this is true! We're not claiming to know what God's ways are. This, however, is only one side of the ledger. We're given Scripture that we might hear God. This is why the reading of Scripture has been so important in Christian history and why the churches of the Reformation place so much emphasis on the teaching of Scripture.

---

5. See Branson, *Memories, Hopes and Conversations*.

6. Bible studies like this abound, but the specific practice of Dwelling in the Word was coined by the Church Innovations Institute in 2008. Learn more at *www.churchinnovations.org*.

God invites us to attend and discern, but in a humble, tentative way. We are like apprentices, together learning a new skill, and in a good apprentice there is little room for arrogance. Our learning may be awkward at first, and we will get things wrong. That's all part of the journey. (Israel discovered this once they crossed the Red Sea; the disciples certainly experienced this when Jesus sent them on their way.) It is why we don't try to do this listening and discernment on our own; we commit to living in a church community, in humble submission to one another.

God's ordinary people discern God's activities in their contexts, and it is important for God's people to recover the practice of listening to God through Scripture.[7] There are, of course, times when a trained person has background knowledge of a Biblical passage, and these brief, well-timed comments can augment the ongoing work of the people. The work of preaching and teaching can only enrich the people's capacity to dwell in the Word. However, we need to challenge the myth that God's plans and initiatives are delivered only by leaders. In that narrative, ordained leaders provide authoritative directions, and ordinary people get aligned with the plan or vision. Instead, Dwelling in the Word is a practice in which God's ordinary people become the listeners to the ways of God in their local contexts. The more this happens, the more confident people become in testing this listening in their own neighborhoods.

As Dwelling in the Word is not chiefly the work of leaders, it is also different from the practice of Bible study. In Bible study we analyze a passage in order to get at its basic meaning. Usually such analysis depends on study guides, commentaries, and teaching summaries. The goal is to get a clear understanding of what the text was intended to say and, sometimes, how we can apply it to our lives. This is important work in any community. A good understanding of meaning, context, language, and history is helpful for entering the world of the Bible. But getting the right knowledge and the right understanding has too often become the end of the process.

Dwelling in the Word is a different practice with different goals and therefore a different method. "Dwelling" suggests "sitting

---

7. The language of *laity* and *clergy* is so laden with presumptions that I am using the phrase "God's ordinary people" in an attempt to capture the sense that it is in the everyday lives of ordinary people that we discern God's work among us.

before" and "living with." Rather than using commentaries and study guides, we bring ourselves and wait (or dwell) before the text together in a spirit of receptivity. Dwelling is not guided by the need to get the text right, as if we were putting together a commentary, but by the desire to listen through one another for how God might be addressing us. We might say Bible study is how *we read* the text; dwelling is letting the text *read us*. Clearly, dwelling involves practicing our way into a new understanding, rather than understanding our way into a new practice.

Dwelling in the Word is the second element in the listening phase.[8] It is intended to create a change in the expectations and practices of people in a congregation. If we are to go lightly in the way of Jesus into our neighborhoods, then we will need to go with the capacity to listen both to our neighbors and to God's presence in the neighborhood. Dwelling is a simple, gentle practice that helps us to be shaped by the question, "What might we be hearing and seeing God doing among us (as a congregation)?" In practicing with this question, we are moving toward the practice of asking, "What might we be hearing and seeing God doing in our neighborhoods?" The shift in imagination we have discussed throughout this book— the movement from church-centered questions to God-centered questions—depends on this kind of listening.

Listening in Our Neighborhood

The third element is listening to our neighbors. God is abundantly and creatively present in our neighborhoods. What we want to do as God's people is practice how to listen in on what God is up to in the neighborhood so we can join God there. If you are seeking to travel lightly with Jesus, begin by practicing the art of listening to the neighborhood.

In my experience most congregations are energized and excited about listening to one another's stories and Dwelling in the Word, but listening in their neighborhoods is a big ask. Here is what happened when Stacey tried it. She is a member of an Episcopal

---

8. For a simple outline of how to go about doing this dwelling process see Practice Guide A on page 68.

congregation in New Jersey where she and others are discovering the practices of listening with one another and their neighborhood:

I've noticed that things look different from the walking versus driving perspective. When I'm walking, I'm part of the neighborhood and notice smells and sights and sounds that surround me. Recently, I walked in the neighborhood with some folks from St. David's. We started out in our parking lot, and before setting off, we prayed for our congregation and our neighborhood. Soon we were next to Terry and Mary's house, where we stopped to pray for Mary's brother Richard, who is dying, and for their family. A little farther up the road, surrounded by the high school, middle school, and elementary school, we prayed again, this time for the children in our community, and for those who guide and teach and care for them. Crossing through the high school property, we found ourselves in front of town hall, where we prayed for our leaders and community. And as we came to the animal shelter and the recycling center, we stopped to pray for God's creatures and all of creation.

I'd never taken a walk like that before. On that day, we were present in the neighborhood. Through this practice I'm beginning to see my neighborhood. Assumptions are falling away. I am not so much seeing the neighborhood differently, as seeing it for the first time. I can't be engaged in the neighborhood from the safety of my car or living room. I've had to leave my comfort zone and my armor.

A story may illustrate what I'm trying to convey. Irene and I live around the corner from each other. We'd gone to church together for four years before we realized we lived in the same neighborhood. One day we decided to take a walk around the lake in our community. It was the 5th of July. We drove to the lake and saw something was going on. There was a crowd of families with young children. Everyone was dressed for July 4th in red, white, and blue. There were kids on bikes, toddlers on tricycles, and babies in carriages. There were dogs with bandanas tied around their necks. Lots of people were waving American flags. We could hear the sound of a fire truck's siren, and it looked like a parade was going on. We decided to follow. After a few minutes, we came to a street corner where a group of neighbors were gathered. Most of them had dogs on leashes, and some were offering plates of food. We stopped and asked what was going on, and they told us that it was the annual 4th of July parade around the lake. Apparently, every year around the 4th, families parade behind the fire truck around the lake and over to the beach, where there are ceremonies and activities all day long. Huh! I'd lived in the neighborhood for ten years and never knew about this!

As we continued along the parade route, I told Irene how hard it had been for me and my kids moving to this neighborhood. As a single mom with a third and fifth grader, I had felt left out and isolated. When I would go to the kids' soccer games, school concerts, or the lake in the summer, none of the other parents talked to me. I felt that I had "missed my chance" because I had not met them and formed friendships when our kids were in kindergarten. I told Irene how hurt I had been, and still was, because I never felt like I really belonged in the community. As I finished telling my tale, we came to another corner and noticed a crowd of people in a driveway. They had a table set up with coffee and juice and donuts; everyone was festively dressed for the 4th. The flag was flying, and music was playing. As it turns out, these neighbors gather every year to celebrate the 4th and to watch the ragtag parade to the beach. Irene recognized some of the people and introduced me. In no time I had met the entire crowd, and Irene shared my story of how I felt so isolated in the community. Several apologized that that had been my experience. I was welcomed into the group, and we ended up spending the next hour celebrating with the crowd. As we were leaving, I was invited to join them on the beach in the evenings to watch the sunset. They said they were there just about every night and would keep an eye out for me. What do you think God was up to in the neighborhood that day?

Many people share Stacey's original experience of alienation, but it hasn't always been true. Not that long ago the neighborhood was the primary place of social life. Not long ago it was possible, when life became a bit crazy, to ask the neighbors next door to keep an eye on the kids while you ran to an appointment or picked up something at the local grocery store. It was once fairly normal when you ran out of potatoes or flour to borrow it from the neighbor. Those days are gone in many places. I was visiting with a pastor recently in a major city who invited me for supper with her family. As we drove into her townhouse complex, we turned into a narrow, empty lane between the two sets of townhouses. The lane was made up of a long series of garage doors on either side. As we approached, one of the doors opened, we turned into the garage, and the door closed automatically behind us. I was aware that the very design of that complex, the buildings themselves, was such that this pastor and her family would have almost no incidental contact with anyone else who lived there. In the midst of such a constructed space, reaching out might be strange or out of place. It is easy to see how we have come to know so little about our neighbors and have so little regular contact with them.

Social researcher Marc Dunkelman writes that, since the 1960s the "social architecture" of North America has been upended and radically transformed. He is referring to the ways we live and relate with one another in our built environments. Most people were part of communities of difference, where people with "different skills and interests, disparate concerns and values, collaborated with their neighbors in pursuit of the common good."[9] Somewhere between the 1950s and 1990s, our day-to-day commerce with one another and basic habits of life were upended to the point where most of us no longer know or engage with people in our neighborhoods. We no longer participate in the everyday messiness of being with people who, in one way or another, are different. Robert Bellah signaled this shift in the 1980s with the book *Habits of the Heart*. In it, his team described the shift away from identities formed in relation with local people and places, and toward a greater individualism that turned away from others across the street, a few doors down, or up a flight of stairs.[10] Thanks to that shift, we developed a new social architecture. We started constructing buildings like the townhouse described above or "single-family dwellings" with fenced backyards and little

9. Dunkelman, *The Vanishing Neighbor*, xvii.
10. Bellah et al., *Habits of the Heart*.

connection with the streets. The new separateness was embedded into the very brick and wood structures we call home.

In a startling assessment, Dunkelman describes how our understanding of "neighborliness" has been transformed:

> During the mid-2000s, two psychiatrists on the faculty of Harvard Medical School, Jacqueline Olds and Richard Schwartz, noted that the definition of "neighborliness" had evolved dramatically over the course of several decades. In the early postwar period, being neighborly meant reaching out to the people who lived next door—taking a homemade cake to the family moving into the house across the street, offering to watch the kids in a pinch, saying hello at an annual block party, or inviting acquaintances to join a Wednesday night bowling league. Over the years, however, the terms came to denote almost exactly the opposite. Today, "being neighborly" means leaving those around you in peace.[11]

Journeying into our neighborhoods in the way of Jesus is truly counter-cultural. It is not a pleasant project to add to the list of other church tasks. We are talking about the transformation of a congregation's self-understanding and practices.

Back when the majority of our congregations were formed, members generally lived in the same neighborhood as their church buildings (and of course, the word "building" was synonymous with the word "church"). There was, then, an organic, rhythmic connection between church and neighborhood. Over the years all that changed, even for those communions that describe churches in terms of "parishes." Following the end of World War II, many people moved out of the communities they and their parents had called home for generations. They filled new housing tracts built along the new interstates spreading out across the continent.

Initially, these families drove back to the church (building) and remained connected to the people of the familiar, old congregation. As time passed, new people moved into the neighborhood, and they weren't connected with the congregation. These new people were different in lots of ways: race, ethnicity, economics, politics. The congregation continued in its ways, but the "kids" were not coming

---

11. Dunkelman, *The Vanishing Neighbor*, 130.

anymore. They had grown up, gotten jobs, formed families of their own, and headed off to new homes ever further away from the old church. These churches became enclaves of like-minded and similar-looking people; they were affinity groups living inside the same social, economic, and language worlds, getting ever older and more separate from the people who now call the neighborhood home.

The call of the Spirit to go and listen in the neighborhoods is a real challenge for many church communities. Reimagining church as more than an affinity group serving people who look, think, and behave like the original members is a huge undertaking.

Because the practice of listening in our neighborhood is a lost art, it will feel awkward at first. When we moved to our current neighborhood, I started hanging out at a local coffee shop to get to know people. It felt strange and awkward. I wanted to go back to my old neighborhood and all the familiar places. That always happens with a new practice. So we have to start slowly and simply. It's amazing how people start to relax, lose their self-consciousness, and have fun. Over the two and a half years we have lived in our neighborhood, walking about and choosing to hang out in places, we have already learned amazing stories about people on the street and its creative history. You can do it, too. Practice Guide B on page 70 offers ways any congregation can start listening in on their neighborhood.

❖ ❖ ❖

These are the three elements that begin our journey: listening to one another, to God, and to the neighborhood. It's not just the listening by itself that's important but the ways in which, through this listening, people keep sharing the stories of what they are observing, discovering, and hearing. Moreover, within these stories we are continually inviting one another to name those places where we might see God at work ahead of us. This ongoing, cumulative process of listening, sharing stories, and reflecting begins to shape an environment where people imagine fresh ways of traveling lightly as followers of Jesus into their neighborhoods.

PRACTICE GUIDE A

Dwelling in the Word

Based on ancient practice, this simple exercise can be used during the first 20–30 minutes of each gathering or meeting.

The specific text we recommend in The Missional Network is Luke 10:1–12. (See my book *Missional: Joining God in the Neighborhood* for an explanation of this text in the context of Luke/Acts.) We believe it expresses what many of us want as God's people in our local church—to empower a movement of men and women who see their neighborhoods and communities as the places of God's life. We are seeking to cultivate a Luke 10 movement across North America.

As you dwell in this text with others, we pray that you will be drawn into the question of how the Spirit might be calling you to enter your neighborhood in a similar manner.

Here is what is involved in Dwelling:

Have copies of the text available for everyone.

> Have two people (male/female) ready to read the passage out loud twice.
>
> After the first reading, ask people to be open to the Spirit through these questions:
>
> > o As the text is read a second time, where do you stop?
> > o Are there words, phrases, or ideas that grasp you?
> > o Is there a question you'd like to ask a New Testament scholar if you could?
>
> After the second reading, invite people to ponder the questions.
>
> Following several minutes of silence, ask people to find someone in the room they do not know and with whom they did not come. Sit in a comfortable place together.
>
> Each gives the other two minutes and listens to where the other person has stopped and how they have responded to one of the questions.

After two minutes switch around and listen to your partner. The purpose here is to listen attentively to what the other person is saying. You may want to ask a question or two, just to understand what he or she is saying, but remember the focus of attention here is this process of listening attentively to the other.

After four or five minutes come back together as a whole group. The leader will ask people to share what they heard their partner saying. Where did they stop in the text and why? How did they hear God? What new insight or question emerged? Again, remember, your role here is to report what you heard the other sharing with you. The attitude is one of focused attention and reporting the words of the other. Resist the temptation to anticipate what your partner will say and stop listening, or to jump in and share your own insightful comments.

At the end of this time, briefly ask the group if there have been any specific ways the Spirit spoke to them through the text.

Finally, ask the group, "How are we hearing God's call to practice Luke 10 in our neighborhoods and communities?"

PRACTICE GUIDE B
Listening to Our Neighborhoods

You are invited to participate in some simple but fresh ways of discovering and listening to your local neighborhood. Many people wonder, "Why do we have to listen to our local neighborhoods?" There are four reasons:

1. Most churches were built in neighborhoods and were designed to be for the neighborhoods in which they were built.

2. Societies have changed and it is no longer normal or natural for people to come to church. The goings-on of a church often do not interest those outside the church, so trying to make church more attractive will not compel people to come.

3. Instead of expecting people to come to our churches, we need to go where they are.

4. We need to learn how to join with what God is doing in our neighborhoods and communities. God's nature is to join us where we are, and we are invited to join others where they are just as God joins us.

You may find the following video helpful in answering the questions about why listening in our neighborhoods is such an important part of this journey. Please feel free to share the video with your congregation. *http://vimeo.com/77079681*

Next, here are some simple tools to assist you in learning how to listen to your neighborhood.

1. Mapping Your Neighborhood
   - Imagine you are in a helicopter looking down on your neighborhood.
   - Draw a sketch of what you see in your mind.
   - What is at the center of your neighborhood? Draw this image.
   - Mark the shopping places, parks, or schools in the neighborhood.
   - What other landmarks do you want to mark? Notice other houses of faith, businesses, fire or police stations.

- Mark the gathering places on your map.
- Mark your favorite place to go in the neighborhood. Consider why you chose this.
- Mark your least favorite place to go in the neighborhood. Consider why you chose this.
- List any major boundaries in your neighborhood, for example, geographic features like rivers, forests, mountains, or hills, or man-made boundaries like railroad tracks, highways, bridges, and freeways.
- Who is in your neighborhood? Are certain sections populated by certain groups?
- Name the people you know in the neighborhood and locate where they live on your map.
- What are some of the stories you could tell about people in the neighborhood?

2. Listening in Your Neighborhood

Aim to eventually walk around your neighborhood three or four times a week. Do this at different times of the day: early in the morning, early afternoon, late afternoon, and early evening. Here are some questions to reflect on:

- What does your neighborhood look like (buildings, parks, apartments, etc.)?
- Are different people, groups, events, or gatherings at these different times?
- What would this community look like at . . .

  o 7 a.m.?
  o Noon?
  o 6 p.m.?
  o 10 p.m.?

- Who is on the street?
- What are people doing?
- Are there things that surprise you?
- What raises your curiosity?

- What creates concern or questions?
- Is there anything that catches your attention in a way that you want to ask more questions or get more information?

Go for a 45-minute walk and try out these observation questions; combine your looking with some demographic research or talking with people who know the neighborhood's history and present.

- What kinds of residences have been built? Why might your neighborhood have been built the way it was?
- How long ago was it developed?
- Do the original people still live here? If not, where did they go? Why?
- Who are the people groups here? Where did they come from? How long have they been here?
- Who is invisible? Why?
- Where are the differences and stress points in this community? How is difference dealt with?
- How does communication take place? Where is the church being heard (if at all)?
- What do the primary organizations and services tell you about the area?
- Who are the individuals who connect and bridge in this community?
- Who do you know in the neighborhood? Why do you know these specific people? What makes them unique? What stories can you tell about them?
- What three things would you do to improve your neighborhood?

Use all of your senses as you "listen" to the neighborhood:

- What do you see? Not see?
- What do you smell? Not smell?
- What do you hear? Not hear?
- What do you feel? Not feel?
- What effect did any of these things have on you?
- Did you stop to listen to anyone on your walks?

Notice ways people gather and connect in your community:

- Young parents may meet in certain spaces. What are they discussing? Perhaps you could join them.
- Seniors gather regularly in certain areas to talk with each other. They are open and eager for others to join in and listen to their stories. What are they sharing?
- Teens and younger adults often communicate via text message or social media (Facebook, Instagram, Twitter, etc.). How might you join the conversation? What are the issues and themes these generations are addressing?
- Where are the local gathering spots in the area? Who gathers there? What would be involved in hanging out there sometimes?
- What local stores get the most business? What is happening?
- Who gathers at the bus stop each morning?
- Where are the clubs, gyms, community centers, or other local places people gather?

Listening Summary:

- What am I learning about my neighborhood?
- What am I learning about my engagement in my neighborhood?
- What am I learning about my church's relationship to my neighborhood?

CHAPTER SEVEN

Practice 2—Discerning

It seemed good to the Holy Spirit and to us . . .

—Acts 15:28

The next practice of the journey is *discernment.* A congregation's vocation is to discern the ways the Spirit is continually inviting it to join with God in their neighborhoods. If you take on the practices of listening described in chapter six, you will have plenty of experiences around which to discern.

Discernment is a big word that can be either scary or cliché for congregations. It's truly about bringing God back into the center of our conversations and actions. This is the practice by which a congregation develops the capacity to name concrete ways they might join with God in their neighborhoods. Discernment is different from analyzing a neighborhood and then deciding how to meet some related need. Such research and response is not wrong, nor is helping others an improper form of Christian action. Discernment is simply a different way of seeing and being with your neighborhood.

First, discernment assumes God is already active in the neighborhood. Second, it assumes that listening with our own ears and seeing with our own eyes gives us clues to where God is at work. Third, discernment depends on a willingness to be surprised about the places and among the people where the Spirit might be at work. Fourth, it involves being present without a predetermined strategy for assessment.

Discernment is the way we practice the conviction that the Spirit is already out ahead of us. If this is true, then our common work includes discovering how to listen for what the Spirit is saying to us. Discernment asks the question, "Where might we be seeing God in our neighborhood, and how might we join with God there?"

Challenges to Discernment

The difficulty in developing this practice is that churches have been socialized to work in very different ways. Here are just a couple of the assumptions that make it tough to engage in discernment:

Congregations are organized counter to the practice of discernment.

The people of a congregation have been socialized to be more at home with business meetings with agendas and Robert's Rules of Order, small group gatherings with study guides, or canons and bylaws that determine what can and cannot be done in a congregation and by whom. These practices have their place, but they have squeezed out other practices of listening to God together and asking discernment questions such as, "What does the Spirit seem to be saying to us?" Such questions no longer feel concrete or practical, but out of step with our established ways of being God's people.

The point is that congregations are no longer organized to practice discernment, outside of prescribed processes for discerning ordained vocations. Just as the idea of being a neighbor has been transformed into the opposite of what was intended, so the understanding of how a congregation listens to and discerns God's purposes has also been dramatically upended. Little attention is given to the kind of discernment described here. Our default mode reflects the belief that rules of order, meetings, and bylaws are the primary, concrete ways we know what God wants of us. Discernment can seem a strange, naive prospect.

Congregations see discernment as the individual work of a few "spiritual" people.

I listened in on a conversation in the living room where our little church was meeting. Andy had done a good job introducing Dwelling in the Word as a new way of listening to Scripture. As people responded to the question, "Where do we sense God speaking to us in this text?", it became clear that some in our midst thought they were not qualified to answer. They thought discernment was the work of special, "spiritual" people and not the ordinary, workaday folk sitting in the room that Sunday morning.

Furthermore—again, apart from the work of a Discernment Committee helping a possible candidate for ordination—discernment is generally not understood as a corporate practice we do together, but as a private, meditative activity within oneself.

It's smart to keep these challenges in mind as we seek to form a people practicing the way of Jesus in their neighborhoods. Practicing communal discernment—learning to ask where and how we see God present in our listening practices—is crucial for this journey with Jesus.

The Basics of Discernment

As you shift from listening to discernment, begin asking questions like these:

- Based on the listening we are doing, where might the Spirit be inviting us to join with God in our neighborhoods?
- Are there some concrete steps we can take to test out this sense of the Spirit's invitation?

Initially, these questions may feel disorienting. The usual response is to look at what's happening in a neighborhood and to respond with a project or program. But we want to cultivate a new practice: learning to "see" what God might be doing in the midst of the many good things that are happening. As followers of the way of Jesus, we're learning how to develop the eyes that can see where God is ahead of us in our neighborhoods.

There isn't a formula for discernment. It happens in moments and activities like these:

- listening to one another's stories
- praying together
- Dwelling in the Word
- sharing silence
- worshiping together

All these help a congregation to tentatively propose where we might be sensing the tug of the Spirit in the midst of our listening engagements in the neighborhood.

Discernment, by its very nature, is going to be tentative. It is framed with these kinds of statements:

- "I have an inkling that . . ."
- "I wonder if this might be a place where the Spirit is nudging me to . . . ?"
- "I've seen these new folk in the neighborhood and would really like to . . ."
- "For a long time I've had this sense that I should . . ."

In each of these illustrations there is neither certainty nor guaranteed steps but, rather, this nudging and tentative sense that there are places where we might want to experiment in testing if this is where the Spirit is calling us. Such testing and practicing where God might be calling us comes out of a conviction that God is up to something in the ordinary, concrete, everydayness of our lives. Without this core practice of a Christian community, we have nothing to bring with us into our communities.

Practice Guide C offers some simple activities a congregation can engage to develop the practice of discernment together. These activities are based upon the practices that are developed in Practice Guides A and B; they are not intended to stand apart from the important, initial work of listening to each other, to God, and to our neighborhoods.

PRACTICE GUIDE C

Discernment Gatherings

Using the listening practices you have already tried out, form a series of Discerning Teams that will come together on at least four occasions. The rhythm of these meetings should be quite simple. Below is a suggested overview of the agenda, based on a two-hour evening meeting that ideally includes a meal so you can gather to pray, eat, and work around a table.

Prior to your meeting, invite everyone to engage the chart below.

FOR DISCERNMENT: WHERE MIGHT WE SEE GOD AT WORK IN OUR NEIGHBORHOODS?	
Question 1: From your neighborhood listening, list some places, things, moments, or connections that have drawn your attention and imagination.	
Question 2: Do any stories, images, or conversations connect with your responses to Question 1, helping to explain why they caught your attention?	
Question 3: Share a little of why these particular things have caught your attention.	
Question 4: Write a brief sentence describing why you think the Spirit is nudging you in these directions.	

Let people know this is an invitation to everyone to share some tentative response at the first meeting.

Meeting 1

Gathering   15 minutes

Sharing around the question: 20 minutes

  Where have I seen God in my life or neighborhood this week?

Dwelling in the Word: Luke 10:1–12   30 minutes

Share responses to the Discernment Chart.   45 minutes

Close the meeting by praying for all   10 minutes
that has been shared.

Between Meetings 1 and 2

Between the first and second meeting, agree to these actions:

1. Pray for one another around the responses people offered in
   their Discernment Charts.

2. Reflect on your own responses each day by praying in this way:

   - Pray the Lord's Prayer.
   - Remain in silence for a minute or more.
   - Pray this prayer:

     *Lord God, I know that you love me and that you have called
     me to be a part of your people. I desire to listen and hear the
     ways you want to shape me now. As we listen to our neighbor-
     hoods together, confirm in me the next steps I might take. As I
     explore the options before me, help me to listen to you through
     others in my group, and to pay attention to what is in the
     depth of my own heart. In these ways may I hear your call to a
     way of life that allows me to love you and those who are in my
     neighborhood. Amen.*

   - After the prayers, return to silence and pay attention for the
     prodding, voice, or direction of the Spirit. Note anything
     you might want to write down.

Meeting 2

Gathering   15 minutes

Sharing around the question: 25 minutes

  Where have I seen God in my life or neighborhood this week?

Dwelling in the Word: Luke 10:1–12	30 minutes
Share your experience of prayer and listening this week.	40 minutes

    After each person has shared, respond briefly to these questions:

      1. Did we hear any common themes?

      2. Did we hear any concrete directions?

Close the meeting by praying for all that has been shared.	10 minutes

Between Meetings 2 and 3

Between the second and third meeting, agree to these actions:

1. Pray for one another.

2. Tentatively respond to these questions:

    • I sense that one of the places the Spirit is inviting me to join with God in my neighborhood is . . .

    • Some of the ways I can do that are . . .

    • Here is what this might look like over the two or three months . . .

Meeting 3

Gathering	15 minutes
Sharing around the question:	20 minutes

    Where have I seen God in my life or neighborhood this week?

Dwelling in the Word: Luke 10:1–1	20 minutes
Share your responses to the questions provided for the past week.	30 minutes
One by one, affirm and pray for each person's intentions.	35 minutes

CHAPTER EIGHT

Practice 3—Testing and Experimenting

For the things we think we have to learn, before we can do them, we learn by doing them.

—Aristotle, *The Nicomachean Ethics*

The first two practices, *listening* and *discerning*, naturally involve experimenting, because we're testing how to do unfamiliar things. I describe this third practice as *experimenting* because the work of the previous two steps is now turned into some kind of action where we more consciously engage our neighborhood. Experiment communicates that we are testing something we are not entirely sure we know how to do and for which the results are not guaranteed.

The notion of experiment connects well with the conviction that we want to travel lightly in the way of Jesus into the neighborhood. Going lightly means we are laying down some of the instinctive ways we have practiced being present in a community. These default patterns often move us to either do something for the community or find ways to help meet the community's needs (outreach programs, food pantry, charitable giving, etc.). As I have said many times, such actions are important, but going lightly into the neighborhoods looks different.

When Jesus offers the counterintuitive instruction, "Take nothing with you" in Luke 10, he is in part calling disciples to move from doing things *for* people to being *with* people in the neighborhood and receiving *from* them. To the extent we can be with and receive from people in our neighborhoods, we will be participating with the Spirit. In this passage, the seventy disciples go and join in the rhythms of social and work life in the towns and villages to which they are sent. The instructions to take nothing with them are intended to put them in a place where, in one sense, they have nothing to bring except themselves and the gospel. In this posture they join with the life of the households, sitting at their tables, sharing their work, and participating in the rhythms of community. Recall Stacey's story in chapter six, and how she started joining with her neighbors down by the lake; she found new relationships and conversations which, as she continues to learn to listen, help to discern what God might be doing in the midst of this rhythm.

This step in the journey is an experiment because, for most of us, it is quite a different way of thinking about being "church'" and acting as God's people. While helping and serving continue to be significant elements of following Jesus, they can also be barriers that insulate us from actually being with and dwelling with the other. Helping and meeting needs can leave us in the driver's seat as the benefactor. We bring the expertise; we have the resources; our skills are critical to the need of the other. In other words, doing things for others, we stay in control. The Luke 10 invitation is perplexing because it asks us to not be in control. The way of Jesus is about being with the neighbor—not solving problems, but being present.

If our primary motivation and drive is to help, to bring the resources and answers, we are not likely to do much discerning, and we are far less likely to be transformed. One of the core convictions of this book is that the Spirit has been disrupting the Euro-tribal churches in order to invite them to discover fresh ways of joining with what God is doing ahead of them. As we learn to go lightly and to be with the people in our neighborhoods, the Spirit will continually show us how to be church in this changed time and place. Our churches will be remade as we learn to go on this journey.

Does this mean the churches have absolutely nothing to share? There are, of course, many resources and traditions that congregations can bring that sustain, inform, and invite us into ever more helpful ways of being communities of Jesus: Scripture, sacraments, fellowship practices, teachings, and so much more. This is *always* a two-way street. But at this moment in the life of the Euro-tribal churches, we need to balance our primary posture of ecclesiocentrism and discern where the Spirit is calling us to go lightly and participate in the life of the neighborhood. That is why we have to test some actions that take us out of the role of benefactor and put us into a different kind of relationship with people around us.

Try, Try Again

Testing involves a willingness to try and fail. Think of starting a new job, having children, learning a new sport: the only way we get good at things is by trying and failing. This cycle of trying, failing, reflecting, adjusting, and trying again teaches us new ways of "practicing" life. That's the way it has always been.

Cultivating this practice of experimenting proves challenging because congregations have become risk averse. We do not place a positive value on taking risks. Instead, the tendency is to ensure nothing unpredictable or unmanageable happens. A good leader will learn how to gently invite people into opportunities to take small risks by trying out a small experiment. Again, just the use of experiment language is helpful, because it communicates that it is okay if things don't work the way they were planned. In fact, it suggests they probably will not. Likewise, a smart leader will reduce anxiety by communicating that the stakes are not too high, nothing major is changing, and no one's future depends on getting this right. The little experiments with which we begin can't include things like selling the building and developing a new community center—that's betting the house on success, and it's too much at this stage.

When my trainer Lucy asks me to do some new exercise, she doesn't make a big deal out of it. In fact she does the opposite. Recently, she introduced a new balance board far more complex than any I had used before. The balance movement wasn't just side-to-side but multi-directional. After I spent a minute weaving all over and falling off, we moved on to something I could do well. A bit later we came back to the board and, gradually, I started to experience success. Lucy's secret: she didn't pressure me to succeed at the outset. Experiments are all about creating small steps where people start to test and risk being with and participating with others, growing their capacity as they continue discerning what God is up to in their neighborhood.

At Northside Baptist Church in Clinton, Mississippi, pastor Stan Wilson looked at how he might introduce members of his middle-class, well-educated, liberal congregation to this practice of being with people in the community. He knew the wonderful ways these good people had given their time and energy in projects doing good for others. He now wanted to invite them into another way of doing and seeing, one that recognizes the dignity, worth, and agency of all. "Until we can say to someone that we value their person above their achievements, standing, or wealth, then there is no reason for them to trust us. Until we value someone intrinsically for their own sake, any efforts to 'work for' or even 'work with' another only reveal that we may be using someone in need as a means toward some further end."[1]

As part of learning this new practice, Stan sought low-risk ways for them to "try on" new behaviors. He invited some members to continue practices of Dwelling in the Word and daily prayer. He also introduced the notion of a "third place" and invited them to simply find such a place in their neighborhood and begin to get to know people there. (Ray Oldenburg coined the term "third place" to indicate any place beyond home and work where informal social gatherings can be hosted.[2]) To help with this experiment, they were given a simple exercise and question: "As you walk about your neighborhood, where do you see people gathering outside of home or work? Make plans to hang out in that place on a regular basis over the next several months." This hanging out involved learning to participate in informal conversations with people and listening to their stories without needing to offer solutions or bring any help. As they met others, they might ask simple questions like, "How long have you lived in the neighborhood?" or "What do you like best about this community?" The group then met weekly to share what they were discovering in the practice of inhabiting a third place.

All this was new for members of Stan's church, so they had to stretch outside their comfort zones; but they stayed in the familiarity of their neighborhood, so it wasn't too much of a stretch. This is

---

1. See Samuel Wells and Marcia A. Owens, *Living Without Enemies: Being Present in the Midst of Violence* (Downers Grove, IL: InterVarsity Press, 2011), 38.

2. Ray Oldenburg, *The Great Good Place: Cafés, Coffee Shops, Bookstores, Bars, Hair Salons, and Other Hangouts at the Heart of Community* (Cambridge, MA: Da Capo Press, 1999), 14–19.

one characteristic of a good experiment. It invites us to stretch some (risk) but not too much (security). When both elements are held together, the likelihood for new learning is high.

Experiments That Work

Experiments can take so many shapes and cover all sorts of ground (see Practice Guide D for a few more). At one Lutheran congregation, a group has started a community book club with neighbors. Participants choose the books, and meetings happen in people's homes rather than the church building. In another area, a group of church people established a plot in an existing community garden. This shared plot became the space for informal conversations with neighbors. They talked about food and farming and healthy food production. But members also reported that new relationships emerged and that, in the context of their work together, more "God" questions came up than happened at church on Sunday morning.

A suburban church couple realized they simply did not know how to connect with others in their busy neighborhood. Where could they start? What would an experiment even look like? How could they translate Luke 10 into the vernacular of a modern North American suburb? They have a lot of space at the front of their house but no sidewalks or ways of congregating on the street. They took a small strip of land at the side of the house and, in the spring, turned it into a garden. As spring moved into early summer, they put a sign in their experimental garden that said: "We want to share the produce of this little garden with any who wish to enjoy its fruits. Please feel free to take what you would like." To their total surprise, people not only took the produce but turned up at the door to thank them. Conversations began, and soon they had a fresh way of being with their neighbors.

In the introductory chapter, I briefly mentioned an aging church that found new life in the neighborhood. This once-rural congregation found itself surrounded by new housing developments and shopping centers. The members thought new people would flock to the church, but when they didn't, the church folks had to struggle to understand what it meant to be a church in this new context. Through their listening to one another and Dwelling in Luke 10, they decided on an experiment. They now partner with the local community association to plan community events like the association's Winter Festival. This practice of being with people has begun to give them a greater sense of the people now moving into the community. They are making new friends, connecting with people quite different from themselves, and finding that dwelling with the other can be downright fun. They are discovering fresh energy and starting to stretch a bit more and to imagine other ways of being a part of the developing neighborhood. In the process, they are imagining ways the Spirit might be nudging them to be a different kind of church.

These simple experiments in joining God in the neighborhood aren't major undertakings, do not require a large outlay of cash, and do not require complex, high-maintenance activities over a long period of time. The best experiments are simple and don't cost anything. Such experiments are always shaped by the listening and discerning practices. Their purpose is to give people simple, low-threshold ways of discovering what God might be doing and joining God. The more people take these small steps, the more they see opportunities they hadn't seen before and start waking up to where God is already present in the neighborhood.

Over time working with congregations and listening to their stories, I've seen the characteristics of good experiments. They tend to be:

- Simple, easy to do, not complicated, like spending a couple of hours a week hanging out at the local coffee shop
- Light on structure and organization, like participating in a book club
- Open ended and not loaded down with preconceived outcomes. People (especially church people) expect to be surprised and to learn.
- Free of expert or professional support
- Open to the possibility of failing
- Challenging, that is, they move us out of comfortable, expected roles
- More focused on listening than telling or doing
- Open to partnership with neighbors
- Full of opportunities to listen to the Spirit

Experiments tend to be less than helpful when they:

- Leave church people in charge
- Require a significant budget
- Are complex
- Solve a problem
- Have a pre-planned, expected outcome
- Come with "high stakes"
- Address structural or organizational change
- Aim at recruiting new members to your church
- Aim at meeting needs

You'll know you've been successful at an experiment as you answer questions like these:

- As we join with people in our neighborhood, are we seeing fresh ways God is already at work? What are we seeing?
- Are we being transformed by this experience? What is changing in us?
- Are we discovering how to be church in our communities? What are we discovering?

Experimenting gets churches out of the ecclesiocentric default of having all the answers, all the resources, all the control. God is ahead of us, and our churches are remade and communities change as we participate with God. Taking these small steps can lead to a huge impact.

PRACTICE GUIDE D

Sample Experiments

Read these accounts and consider where you see elements of good experiments and how one foray leads to another.

Characteristic of a Good Experiment

To refresh, here are the characteristics of a good experiment from page 86.

- Simple, easy to do, not complicated, like spending a couple of hours a week hanging out at the local coffee shop
- Light on structure and organization, like participating in a book club
- Open ended and not loaded down with preconceived outcomes. People (especially church people) expect to be surprised and to learn.
- Free of expert or professional support
- Open to the possibility of failing
- Challenging, that is, they move us out of comfortable, expected roles
- More focused on listening than telling or doing
- Open to partnership with neighbors
- Full of opportunities to listen to the Spirit

You'll know you've been successful at an experiment as you answer questions like these:

- As we join with people in our neighborhood, are we seeing fresh ways God is already at work? What are we seeing?
- Are we being transformed by this experience? What is changing in us?
- Are we discovering how to be church in our communities? What are we discovering?

The Book Club

A group of women decided to try an experiment where they joined a book club for newcomers to the neighborhood. The books were chosen by group consensus and represented a wide range of literature. As they met month by month, they shared questions about the books and through that sharing they learned about people's lives and wrestled with meaning. They noticed that the conversations were full of God's presence.

Eventually one of the church women, Mary, hosted the book club at her home. After most people had left, one of the club members, Sally, stayed after the meeting. Sally began to open up to Mary and to share not just her loneliness but that in the economic meltdown, as a single person, she was not making ends meet. In the course of the conversation, Mary wondered if God was up to something, and if God might be nudging her to join in. Even as Sally shared, Mary prayed for guidance, and though she had an early meeting in the morning, she made the decision to give Sally her full attention as she listened to her story.

As their conversation wrapped up, Sally thanked Mary and said she had never felt so supported and heard. Mary noticed the visible relief on Sally's face. Upon later reflection, Mary was amazed and realized she had joined in God's work just by being there for Sally.

Soup Night

Karen had been so focused on the business of church that she didn't know anyone in the neighborhood where she had lived for the past four years. After a time of quiet, silence, Scripture reading, and conversation with trusted friends, she tried an experiment. She was a natural organizer and leader, but her experiment was to spend three to six months participating with people in her neighborhood, listening to them, receiving from them, and seeing what God wanted to do.

She started by letting go of her car, so she had to walk wherever she went in the community. She started bumping into people on a regular basis. Passing conversations began to deepen. She was becoming a regular part of the life of the neighborhood at the ground level.

To further the experiment, she decided to join some groups and clubs. Because she had now turned her attention to her street and, indeed, her own house, she noticed that her back garden was a bit of a mess. She joined a garden club and was stunned by the number of locals from all walks of life. From there, she heard more about issues shaping the area and connected with other groups committed to improving the community.

In the midst of this awakening, Karen's life remained shaped by daily prayer and Scripture (what she would call keeping the Daily Office), and these practices enriched and expanded her new practices of being in the neighborhood. She was genuinely asking, "What is God up to here in my community?" Out of this experiment in being present and dwelling, Karen sensed that a simple thing she could begin to do with her new friends (almost all of whom found the church a strange, alien place) was practice hospitality. She created a monthly soup night for the neighborhood, with an open invitation to her house for supper and conversation. Sometimes a dozen people turn up; sometimes it's twenty or thirty. People share soup, break bread, and talk about life. This is like nothing Karen ever experienced in her many years as a highly involved leader in her church. She is now asking how these God-shaped conversations in her neighborhood shape the way she does church.

CHAPTER NINE

Practice 4—Reflecting

The three practices we've explored so far are essential for congregations learning how to join God, remake their churches, and participate in life- and world-changing ministry. Listening, discerning, and experimenting all help congregations to develop new rhythms of life. Each stretches us because it calls for new learning and practicing new habits. That said, the practice of *reflecting* may be the most difficult and the most important. This is the moment when a congregation starts to self-consciously reflect on what it has done. Without getting the practice of reflection into the bones and rhythms of a congregation's life, the first three practices will be little more than brief excursions. Like the popular "40 Days to . . ." programs, people would be excited for a time, but eventually drop away without any real reflection on what took place and what the next actions might be.

I am a proponent of *action-learning*. First, people simply learn about a new practice; then comes practicing the new practice. Behind it is the conviction that thinking, reading, or attending a workshop alone will not lead us into a new way of being church. We learn and then we apply our learning, acting our way into seeing, thinking, and behaving differently. Each of the practices introduced so far is a step, and we take small steps, test, reflect, learn more, and try again. Remember: John Dewey once said the only experiences we learn from are the experiences we reflect on. This step makes the rest worthwhile.

The simple questions in Practice Guide E provide a pathway for people to reflect on their learning and determine how to take next steps. Without this reflection, the rest of the steps—especially the step of deciding, which comes next—are much more difficult.

PRACTICE GUIDE E
A Pattern for Reflection

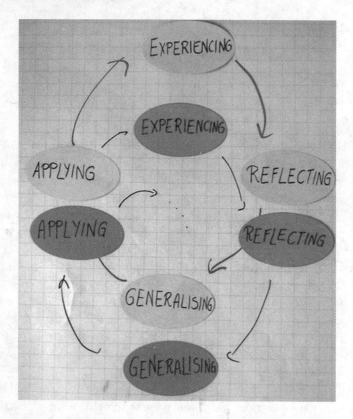

The practice of reflection has several components and each is important. The pattern of reflection is as follows:

1. *What have we done?* Share together what you have done:

    a. Is there a story that best captures your experience?
    b. What did you enjoy most about this experience?

2. *What happened?* On the basis of what you have done, ask:

    a. In what ways did you experience God at work in all this?
    b. How have your attitudes toward this journey changed? Why?

    c. How have your assumptions about being church been challenged?

    d. What has worked well? Why?

    e. What didn't work well? Why?

3. *So what?* What are you learning about:

    a. Listening to God in the neighborhood?

    b. Traveling lightly?

    c. Being *with* rather than doing *for*?

4. *New questions:* What new questions are emerging from these experiences, especially in relation to:

    a. Your sense of listening to the Spirit?

    b. Being church in your neighborhood?

    c. Are there now new ways you want to imagine being church together?

5. *Key takeaways:* What are the key things you want to share with the rest of the congregation?

CHAPTER TEN

Practice 5—Deciding

The fifth practice for the journey of reframing the churches' imagination from ecclesiocentric to God-centered—that is, traveling lightly with Jesus into our neighborhoods—involves making a *decision*. Based on the listening, discerning, experimenting, and reflecting you've done so far, you can now decide how to initiate a new set of experiments.

A small number of people in a congregation have usually been engaged in the first four practices, and even for them the practices are sure to still seem new. I am reminded of the wisdom of my trainer, Lucy, and how she introduces me to a new set of exercises designed to strengthen and stabilize my core. The first time I have to concentrate hard. When I come back to the exercises a week later, it's not as if they magically feel like a normal part of the way my body operates. Quite often, Lucy has to show me the exercise again; then, after a few tries, I get a better feel for them. This is where you are on the journey—the moment for moving deeper in the journey, with a few more people and a little experience under your belt.

Is it time to go further? First, the congregation must engage the practice of deciding. This step is critical for churches as they build on the first round of practices.

PRACTICE GUIDE F

Coming to Decision

1. The Leader's Role

The pastoral leader needs to step up and curate the process of deciding. The skill needed here is knowing the difference between making decisions for the congregation and ensuring that the congregation makes the decisions. Curating is guiding a process in which others make the decisions for themselves. If the minister proposes recommendations, people will generally agree, but they will not own them in the long run. Curating involves creating spaces for interacting, listening, sharing, and making decisions the people can own and invest in implementing.

2. The Plan

Think through the various steps necessary for people to make decisions well. Don't create vague, general bullet-point agendas, but work at developing good process agendas for each step. Remember there are three important decisions to be made:

a. First, the congregation as a whole should hear the stories of what has happened and then decide this is a direction they all want to keep moving.

b. Second, another small number of people need to decide to engage the journey of listening, discerning, experimenting, and reflecting.

c. Third, those in the first group need to decide how they will continue this journey into their neighborhoods.

3. The Communication

Gather the fruits of the reflection process outlined in chapter nine and craft a communication piece for the key leaders of the congregation. A wise leader will see that the structure of that communication piece is already provided in the points outlined in the reflection chapter. To refresh, those points are:

- What have we done?
- What happened?
- So what?
- New questions
- Key takeaways

This outline is a fine frame for the communications piece. In addition, you should apply these guidelines for telling the story of the journey so far:

a. Involve those who participated in this first group.
b. Make it as interactive as possible.
c. Provide a picture of the journey of going lightly in the way of Jesus into the neighborhood.
d. Share the five key practices (listening, discerning, experimenting, reflecting, and deciding) and why they are important.
e. Emphasize that these practices should become part of the congregation's life, not stand alone as another program.

4. Gathering the Leaders

Gather those who have been on the journey with the elected leadership and key leaders, and facilitate a meeting that includes the following:

a. Sharing the communications piece described above
b. Listening carefully to their questions and, along with others who engaged the process, take time to interact around these questions
c. Proposing a time for gathering with the whole congregation to share this communication, and inviting others to join in the journey of discerning and experimenting

5. Gathering the Church

Bring the congregation together for a dedicated gathering time to do the following:

a. Share the communications piece

b. Tell the stories

c. Share a picture of what God is doing; using stories from your own and other congregations, offer a picture of how the future could look

d. Listen to people's responses

e. Continue to communicate that no structures, programs, or roles are being changed—things in the church continue as they have been. This journey is about listening and experimenting, and includes time to stop and reflect on what is happening.

f. Depending on your congregation's decision-making processes, either members present for this gathering should have a chance to officially affirm the direction and the launch of a new cycle in the journey, or the leadership body should reconvene as soon as possible to decide.

6. Next Steps

- Set a date for beginning the next round of listening, discerning, experimenting, and reflecting. Invite all who are interested to join.

- Reconvene the group from the first round. Ask them to serve as coaches for the new group, and invite them to decide how else they would like to continue their journey.

- Continue communicating with the congregation the steps being taken and keep inviting people to share the stories of their experiences on the journey.

CHAPTER ELEVEN

Bypassing the Roadblocks

People love to have lived a great story, but few people like the work it takes to make it happen.

—Donald Miller, *A Million Miles in a Thousand Years*[1]

his book has proposed that the great unraveling of the Euro-tribal
churches over the last fifty or more years has actually been none
other than the work of the Spirit. God has used this disruption
to invite churches to change their basic imagination about who they
are and what God is seeking to form in them. To a great extent these
churches have failed to hear the invitation. Indeed, practically all their
actions to undo or fix the unraveling expose an underlying conviction
that human skill, ingenuity, and technique are the primary keys to
changing course. A deeply embedded, default ecclesiocentrism and
clericalism has misdirected the churches' energies.

In the midst of this reality, the Spirit continues to invite us onto a
different journey. Rather than asking, "How do we fix the church and
make it work again?", we are being called to ask, "How do we go on
a journey together, discerning what God is up to ahead of us in our
neighborhoods in order to join with God there?" The Euro-tribal
churches *are* hearing this invitation; we see it in examples of individual
congregations and regional groups, and even in denominations, as with
The Episcopal Church's recent efforts to discover how members and
churches might go lightly in the way of Jesus into the neighborhoods.

The dry bones are being called back to life. This is not an Exile
time, but an Exodus moment. God is acting amongst us, and it has
everything to do with the healing of the world. First, we have to take
our eyes and preoccupation off the church and turn to see the Spirit

---

1. Donald Miller, *A Million Miles in a Thousand Years* (Nashville: Thomas Nelson Publishing, 2009), 96.

out ahead of us. This turn is not denying the importance and the central role of the church in the economy of God. If anything, this is the way we will discover the fresh shape of the churches. Our worship life and our life together as communities of witness must increasingly be informed and shaped by this other journey, just as Israel's life was formed and shaped on its journey.

It is in this context that the Luke 10:1–12 passage starts to make sense. The passage points us beyond ourselves; it calls us to lay down our baggage, our sense of being benefactors in control of outcomes. The passage invites us to go and learn to dwell with others in our neighborhoods. In such dwelling, we can discern the shapes our churches will need to take.

Be Ready: Defaults and Roadblocks

Everyone who has ever set out on a journey with God knows several things are bound to happen. First, the new journey is exciting and energizing. Second, as Israel discovered once it crossed the Red Sea, the established habits, patterns, and values quickly resurface as we journey in untested territory. I have called them "defaults," and make no mistake, they are powerful and go deep.

Defaults operate in the background of every system, unseen but determining our actions. Jeff Madrick, a professor, researcher, and economics writer, recently published the book *Seven Bad Ideas: How Mainstream Economists Have Damaged America and the World*.[2] He says the defaults embedded in the training of mainline economists for more than a generation made them blind to the economic realities leading up to the 2008 economic meltdown. Madrick points to an interview the late Milton Friedman (the godfather of the prevailing laissez-faire theory) gave to television journalist Charlie Rose shortly before his death. In it, Friedman said: "The stability of the economy is greater than it has ever been in our history; we really are in remarkably good shape. It's amazing that people go around and write stories about how bad the economy is, how it's in trouble."[3]

---

2. Jeff Madrick, *Seven Bad Ideas: How Mainstream Economists Have Damaged America and the World* (New York: Alfred A. Knopf, 2014).

3. Ibid., 5.

This illustrates not only how defaults keep shaping our vision, no matter what is in front of us. It also indicates how difficult it is to change people's imagination and cultivate the spaces where they might learn new practices that help them to see the world differently. Most change processes fail because they do not understand or take into consideration the power of such defaults.

In my thirties and forties, I would think nothing of a fast six- or ten-mile run several times a week. Last year, firmly ensconced in my sixties, I told my trainer Lucy I want to train for a six-mile race over the next six months. Lucy smiled, gently, and said: "Let's begin, slowly, and see what happens." She noticed my facial response and continued: "What happens with running more than any other sport is that it quickly brings out underlying conditions beneath the surface in your body." Lucy gave me a six-month training program to gently get me ready for a five-kilometer (about three-mile) race in the spring. I thought I was ready for this adventure, so I began with a 5K once a week then moved to 5K runs three times a week (with requisite days off and alternating cross-training). Three months in, the underlying conditions in my old body manifested. Taken together they shut down my running for several months. I didn't realize I have to practice new exercises every day to gradually move bones back into alignment and stretch muscles that thought they'd been put into retirement.

My point is this: it's one thing to hear the call, but this journey will challenge a lot of underlying habits, practices, and values. Be ready. Journeying lightly in the way of Jesus into our neighborhoods is a massive transition. While our churches are important, today they are neither the only nor the primary places where God is acting. This is highly disorienting because everything about Christian life has said the place where we find God is in a church, either in a building or a worship service, or deep inside the privacy of our own experience. Without denying God's presence in these places, in the midst of our unraveling, we are being called on a Red Sea journey beyond these spaces.

This journey will take courage, wisdom, and partnership. It can't be undertaken alone. It will require a willingness from leaders to learn new skills and risk learning to lead outside established comfort zones. This final chapter touches on some of the powerful, underlying defaults that leaders need to see clearly before setting out. We have to both celebrate what the Spirit is up to ahead of us and be clear-sighted about the challenges.

Identify the Defaults

Congregations are amazingly complex. They don't just line up and follow because you dangle an assessment or vision before them. They're conserving organisms that give a high value to keeping things as they are, even as they speak of the need for change. You have no doubt seen it happen. A leader reads a new book or report and gets excited. He or she excitedly invites the congregation to read it, too. They plan to introduce a congregational study, perhaps in Lent, and perhaps draft a new vision during the season of Easter and launch a new ministry at Pentecost. The usual volunteers get involved, but otherwise there's not much traction.

It's a common story. There are massive defaults at work. The practices described throughout part II are carefully designed to engage these defaults, but leaders need to be aware of the defaults to see how to gently and slowly engage them. What follows is a summary list of the defaults you are most likely to encounter.

I. God is not really acting among us.

While most in a congregation have some vague sense that God is present in the liturgy and their worship life, the conviction permeating this book—that God is actively and present in a congregation and out ahead in their neighborhoods—is an alien idea to most people. Talking in this way is a bit like asking people to describe the taste of a hot, summer's day. These concepts just don't go together.

Talk about God as the active, primary agent in our neighborhoods is disorienting. Many people do not know what to do with it because it is not a recognized part of their experience. Often more "liberal" Christians get nervous because it sounds like God is an anthropomorphic figure who reaches in and sorts things out. This begs all kinds of questions, like why God doesn't stop wars, protect victims of abuse, and more. All these misgivings play out when you ask people to connect with their neighborhoods. They default to making assessments, talking to experts, and figuring out how to meet needs. In the end, God is not active; we are.

This roadblock must be recognized from the beginning in order to be patient with people and recognize that it will take time to enter into this way of seeing. In the practices of listening, dwelling, and discerning, people are being gently invited into a space where together they discover and affirm this new reality. God is active. God is present. God is out there, waiting for us to join God.

II. We cannot experience God through Scripture.

The practice of Dwelling in the Word is becoming popular in many churches. It is based on the conviction that as God's people sit before Scripture—not just listening to a professional preach or teach, but dwelling together—they are in a place where the Spirit speaks to them. In my experience, few Euro-tribal congregations actively assume that God speaks to us in unique, specific ways through Scripture. There is little experience of Scripture as a location where we encounter God; it's usually the source of ideas and concepts about God, or perhaps for inspiration. This is not a criticism or judgment; knowledge and inspiration are vital for a full life of faith. But this powerful default tends to blot out the openness to encounter with God. That is why I introduced the practice of Dwelling in the Word in chapter six and followed with a simple pattern for listening to each other and to the Word.

III. We don't have enough people to take this risk; we won't survive.

This is a tough default to dislodge. The fear of scarcity runs deep. It is exacerbated by the notion that congregations of older people will not survive (a shame, since any reading of the Scriptures confirms that God's future turns up in the very places everyone else has given up on). One of the ways to counteract this default is to invite several congregations to join this journey together. Luke 10 says the disciples went in pairs. For today's churches, going in pairs might mean joining up with other congregations to work on the practices outlined in part II. There will be plenty of stories to share, and plenty of opportunities to see that God really is at work among us.

IV. We have to get our house in order first.

Of course this response comes out of the fear and anxiety of loss, including the loss of control. That does not make it any less palpable and real. That is why I have underlined the need to start slow and start small. Set up little demonstration plots of these practices in the church while letting others tend the work of keeping "the house in order." The excitement and energy of people telling stories about hearing God in fresh ways and being with the Spirit in the neighborhood will gradually turn the anxieties into hope and show others the risks may be worth it.

V. We did not come to church to change the world.

As a pastor for more than twenty-five years, I have learned that while people have many reasons for belonging to congregations, changing the world isn't even in the Top 10. This is not a critical or negative statement. Recognizing it helps us to be realistic and practice this principle: Start where people are, not where you want them to be. Clergy tend to want people to be further along (or closer to their own position). Most of the time, when a leader gives people a vision, however hopeful, it communicates that they're still not good enough and they need to change. None of us likes to hear this. And while you don't intend to judge, this kind of communication feels harsh.

Becoming a congregation shaped by the way of Jesus, going lightly into their neighborhoods is a wonderful vision. It "sings" when added to a mission statement or ensconced in a congregation's value statements. Clergy live for these ideals. Most of us don't join a congregation because of its vision statement or calls to follow some movement involving neighborhoods and the way of Jesus. Most of us are in church, week by week, because the liturgy encourages and strengthens us in our personal lives. We come because singing in the choir is the one place where we find community and creativity. We come because, when we were in crisis years earlier, someone cared for us and it made all the difference. We come because family is there or the clergy person is caring or the sermons are thought-provoking. We come because deep down, we are just plain hungry for God, and the bread and wine feed and sustain us like nothing else.

We come for a long list of reasons, and they ought not be spurned or devalued. These are essential, life-giving practices. I have tried to suggest how the five practices (listening, discerning, experimenting, reflecting, and deciding) can be shaped to honor where people are and give them some gentle steps to test yet another part of the journey with God: the journey into the neighborhood.

VI. What's wrong with meeting needs and helping people?

A characteristic default of every congregation I have seen start this journey is to automatically see their neighborhoods as places where they can do things for people. It is almost an article of faith: "To be with people as a church member is to find ways of helping them and meeting their needs. If we do not do this, we are not Christians." The notion of dwelling with the neighbor, of being *with* rather than doing *for*, feels uncomfortable and less than compassionate. On another level, it is disorienting because people feel they are in control and can manage a project if they are doing something for people. The idea of *being with* leaves people feeling vulnerable.

Getting at this default is like crossing the Red Sea. The five-fold process in part II offers a way of challenging this default. You invite a small group to test ways of dwelling with neighbors and listening to where God is present, and invite other members to reflect and listen at a safer distance.

VII. The clergy should take care of this.

To the extent that clergy lead change, there will be no change. I admit this statement sounds extreme. First, this doesn't mean clergy are unimportant or have no role. It does mean some of the usual assumptions about their leadership need to change. Regardless of theology (lay empowerment, priesthood of all believers, etc.), congregations tend to defer to the presence of clergy. Church is their professional job, or the job for which they've trained and been selected by the church and by God. As in medicine, law, or automobile repair, we respect the knowledge of experts. Observe, for example, what normally happens when clergy sit in on a meeting.

Even when they are not chairing the meeting, people around the table often defer to them in discussion and decision making. Perhaps for this reason, clergy more often than not initiate proposals for action.

There is a simple rule around leadership: When innovators innovate, there will be no innovation. It is counterintuitive, but when clergy function as innovators, they actually foster a culture that shuts down the innovation of others. My observation in working with countless clergy and congregations is that the clergy propose innovations and the members of the congregation either become the worker bees for the innovation or passively (and sometimes passive-aggressively) let them drop.

Congregations have been socialized to follow the initiatives of their clergy, looking to them for direction in terms of projects and actions. This is why initiatives last about as long as the particular clergy person's tenure, then gradually die off or get owned by a small number of people. I call this "elastic band leadership," and it can be illustrated in the following exercise. If you take an elastic band between the fingers of your two hands and stretch it, the band stays taut as long as you hold your fingers in that position. When you remove a finger, the elastic goes back to its original position. The same is true when clergy provide the initiative and innovation.

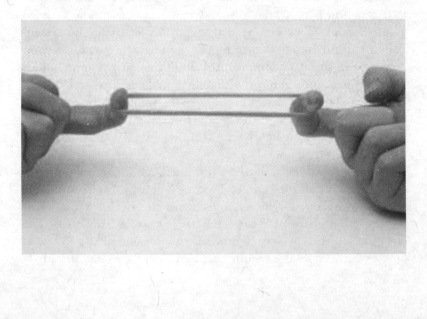

The challenge is to create a congregational culture where innovation isn't driven by or dependent on clergy. Without shared passion, the journey into the neighborhood in the way of Jesus will be little more than one more episodic program the latest pastor introduced. Each of the practices in part II offers a way to lead without having clergy act as the primary innovators.

VIII. We're a caring family; isn't that enough?

Listen closely for how people describe their churches, and you will hear words like "family," "community," "caring," and "loving." This is not the primary language of our theology or confessions about the nature and purpose of the church. We may say, for example, the congregation is called for the sake of the world and sent into the world as agents of God's mission. Or we may declare that a congregation does not live for itself but for the stranger, the other. There is a chasm between statements of belief (what we call "ideational values") and the actual language people use to name their experiences. They understand and experience themselves coming together to support, care for, and watch over each other like a family.

"Family" is a powerful image. In this case, it is a profound default suggesting a group of closely connected people with lots in common. Families spend time together. Families have internalized common habits, practices, and values that they now take for granted. Families are kin. Seen through this lens, church is essentially an affinity group shaped by common habits rooted in a common ethnic, social, or class identity and experience. Communities like this offer much in terms of stability, predictability, and care for one's own. They effectively pass life-giving traditions from generation to generation. But if the goal is to be a people formed in the way of Jesus, traveling lightly into their neighborhoods, this default is a significant roadblock.

Truth be told, most of us are not interested in joining someone else's close-knit affinity group. That may be why Paul continually pleaded with the young church to recognize that in Christ, the "Gentile" is no longer required to become a "Jew" (Galatians 2:14). The story of Cornelius in Acts 10 makes the same point. The good news of Jesus Christ does not require that I join someone else's affinity or ethnic group; the good news connects us across those groupings and makes us one in Christ.

This wisdom gets more important because most of us live in neighborhoods that, increasingly, are populated by people who are not like us. That is true whether you are a primarily black church in an emerging Latino neighborhood, or a church of (once) young families that's now surrounded by singles who won't have children for another ten years, if at all. On some level, we all enjoy the comfort of our affinity groups, but the journey of joining with God calls for a huge transformation of a congregation's self-understanding, habits, and practices. The Spirit invites us to do something that few families, or ethnic or affinity groups would choose: to cross group boundaries and enter the lives of the others who are different and, more often than not, have their own our stories, practices, and traditions.

The five practices in part II offer a simple process for starting down this road. They are intended to serve as a map for changing the basic imagination about who the congregation means when it says "we." The five practices are shaped to help a congregation to ask new questions, expand its imagination, and ultimately engage in its own disruptive remaking.

Conclusion

God's abundant Spirit is bringing new life to the church in North America. It looks a lot like the early chapters of Exodus, where God chooses to act in ways no one else could calculate or anticipate. The Exodus story suggests that God is already out ahead of us, across the Red Sea, beckoning us to cross over, to depart from our ecclesiocentrism and share a new adventure in the neighborhood. God is up to something amazingly generative with the Euro-tribal churches. Things are not going to go back to the way they were. That is good news.

Clearly, many surprises await those who seek to engage this journey. It cuts across some of the most deeply held perceptions. Surprises like this await any of us who seek to go lightly in the way of Jesus into our neighborhoods. The journey cuts across some of the deeply held perceptions and habits of congregations. I hope that, by introducing the five simple practices in part II, you see a track congregations can begin to walk as they embark on this journey.

How do we do this? Slowly. With little steps and lots of stopping to reflect on what we're doing and what we're learning. We never do it alone but always with others. This counter-intuitive practice is done in a community of prayer, and it happens as we continue devotion and corporate worship, where the bread and wine continually feed us with the life of Jesus. This is too big a journey and too important a part of the Spirit's disrupting call to be turned into a project we do before taking up something new next year.

If the Euro-tribal churches of North America are to have a future, it will likely depend on journeys like this. Joining God, remaking church, and eventually participating in God's remaking of the world means leaving our baggage behind and letting go of the things that help to keep us in control, manage the situation, or determine the outcomes we want. Community studies, meeting needs, helping people, and getting expert information are all "baggage" that get in the way of the listening the Spirit wants us to do.

We may think we need more skill, more people, or that we need to get our houses in order. Surely God does not want us when things have unraveled like this. But the Spirit has always called followers in just this situation out on a new adventure. It wouldn't be the strategy I would use. I would find the best and the brightest and make them the center of a new future. I would want to turn a page, move away from the old and seemingly useless to start all over again. But that's not how God's Spirit changes the world. If it was, who among us could stand?

I cannot see any other place on this earth from which the fresh future of God's remaking of the world will emerge, except from congregations. So we take this journey in small steps. We start where people are, inviting them into small experiments that gently draw them out into spaces of risk where the Spirit is to be found. There is no other way. Together, they craft simple activities for listening to God and each other, discerning where they hear the Spirit, experimenting in the neighborhood, and reflecting on what they've seen and done. Then they make the decision to stay on the journey. When people start doing this, it's extraordinary what happens.

Isaiah's invitation from my introductory chapter rings more true than ever:

> Awake, awake
> put on your strength, Zion!
> Put on your splendid clothing,
> Jerusalem, you holy city . . .
>
> How beautiful upon the mountains
> are the feet of a messenger
> who proclaims peace,
> who brings good news,
> who proclaims salvation,
> who says to Zion, "Your God rules!"
>
> (Isaiah 52:1, 7)[1]

---

1. *Common English Bible.*

It's time to try a different journey. There is no future in working harder to fix the unraveling. We are being invited to put on new clothes, to dress for a journey of hope and life. Our Lord is out ahead of us doing new things, and we are, indeed, amazed.